THE HISTORY OF
Champagne

DOM PERIGNON

CELLERÍER

DE

L'ABBAYE D'HAUTVILLERS

1638 - 1715

THE HISTORY OF
CHAMPAGNE

ANDRÉ L. SIMON

WITH 7 COLOUR PHOTOGRAPHS BY PERCY HENNELL
2 MAPS AND 53 DECORATIONS

OCTOPUS BOOKS LIMITED
London · New York · Sydney · Hong Kong

Originally designed and produced for the Ebury Press by
George Rainbird Ltd, London, England

This edition published 1971 by
Octopus Books Limited
30 Bouverie Street, London EC 4
Second impresion 1972

© George Rainbird Ltd 1962
Printed in Czechoslovakia by Svoboda, Prague
ISBN 7064 0006 2
51645/2

Colour photography by Percy Hennell

Contents

Colour Plates

The engravings used as ornaments throughout this volume

are derived from nineteenth-century editions of

wine books in the library of the author

Maps

at the end of the book

Foreword

THE WORLD IS MADE UP of contrasts – rich and poor, sick and fit, saints and sinners; continents and oceans, great barren icefields at the poles, and tropical forests teeming with life; and in between, the temperate fairway, the home of the fruitful vine since the dawn of civilization.

There are some highly specialized publications giving the names of the ever growing number of different varieties of wine-making grapes, and the acreage of the steadily expanding vineyards of the world; also their yearly yield of grapes and wine. But the quantity of wine there is for us to drink is beyond statisticians and their statistics: nobody can possibly tell what is the proportion of each vintage's wines that will be drunk within a few months, or a few years, maybe many years from their vintage date.

There is a great deal in common between us and our wines. Wines enjoy, just as we do, the gift of life, a loan rather than a gift since it is ours and theirs for a short time only; and all wines are, as we are, liable to sickness and doomed to death. Most wines are also quite ordinary wines, as most of us are quite ordinary people. There are, unfortunately, bad wines, as there are bad people, but not nearly so many as the publicity given to crimes leads one to believe.

Good people, whatever pessimists may say, are the rule, not the exception: and so are good wines. Great men, however, are only too few; and so are great wines. They are the wines made with special care and skill from some particularly fine species of grapes which were grown, picked and pressed in a year when the hours of sunshine and the inches of rain happened to be just right. And most great wines must be given time to become great: there are very few infant prodigies who can play Mozart when six years old, and very few wines are great at birth.

All good people are by no means alike: far from it. They differ in race, strength, age and much else, and the same is true of all good wines: they differ according to the species of grapes from which they are made; according to the nature of the soil of their native vineyards; and according to the incidence of sunshine and rain of their vintage. They differ also according to different methods of vinification. By far the greater proportion of all the world's wines are the so-called beverage wines – red and white wines, and *rosés* – the fermentation of which has been allowed to complete its natural course, unaided and unchecked, so that all the sugar originally in the grape-juice is used up, most of it becoming alcohol, which remains in the wine, the rest of it turning into carbonic acid gas, which loses itself in the air. Claret and Burgundy, red and white Graves, Hocks and Moselles, are the prototypes of beverage wines.

There are also the fortified wines, a small proportion only of the whole, the fermentation of which is checked by the addition of alcohol at an early or late stage, so that they are of greater alcoholic strength than beverage wines. Port, Madeira and Sherry are the prototypes of most fortified wines.

There is yet another category: sparkling wine. Here, the last stage of fermentation takes place after the wine has been bottled, so that the carbonic acid gas cannot escape, remaining in solution in the wine so long as a securely held cork keeps it there. When the cork is removed and the wine is poured out, the gas escapes into the air; in doing so it carries tiny drops of wine to the surface, where they mix with the oxygen of the air to form the characteristic *mousse*, or "bubbles", of sparkling wine. Champagne is the prototype of all sparkling wines.

The making of beverage wines dates back to the dawn of civilization. The history of fortified wines starts with the invention of the still, and that of sparkling wines with the use of the bark of the cork tree for making cork stoppers.

Fortified wines can be made anywhere, but nowhere better than in Spain and Portugal, since the grapes grown in the Jerez country, in the Upper Douro Valley, and on the island of Madeira, are more suitable for the purpose than grapes grown anywhere else. Sparkling wines, likewise, can be made anywhere, but, again, nowhere can they compare with the sparkling wine made in Champagne, where conditions are the most suitable for making this type of wine.

The presence of carbonic acid gas in solution in a wine is not necessarily an advantage: on the contrary, for the great majority of wines it is undesirable. The effect of the gas may be compared to that of a loud pedal; it magnifies and amplifies; it makes the common character of common wines more obvious, and it blurs or distorts the charm of some aristocrats among wines, not only the great Clarets, Burgundies and Hocks, but many others of which the bouquet, body and breed are so admirably balanced but only too easily destroyed. Champagne is the one exception to that rule: it is an aristocrat among wines, but is so gentle and modest that it really needs a touch of the loud pedal to bring out its too discreet bouquet, and to drape its somewhat angular body, without in the least affecting the appeal of its breed.

Many other sparkling wines are made, of course, wherever wine-making grapes grow – some by the same costly method as that used for Champagne, others by cheaper, "short-cut" methods. But though all have the bubbles characteristic of Champagne, in all other respects – body, bouquet, and breed – they are quite different. This is why Champagne holds a unique place among the wines of the world. No other wine enjoys such world-wide acclaim and prestige. To millions of people, many of whom may never have tasted Champagne, the name stands for the most desirable of all wines, something joyful and exciting. They will tell you in New York, for instance, that the morning air in Manhattan, in May, is like Champagne, and somewhat cheaper.

Champagne never can be cheap. It is made from grapes which are dearer than any of the other wine-making grapes, and it requires many more skilled hands than any of the other wines to be brought to perfection.

Over many centuries, the fame of the wines of Champagne was challenged by those of Burgundy, which were not unlike in style. The red wines of

Champagne – still, table wines – were in greater demand than its white sparkling wines right up to the middle of the nineteenth century. White sparkling Champagne wine was first heard of at the time of the Restoration, in London, before it was known in Paris and Versailles, where, however, it became very fashionable soon after, though for a short while only. It made little progress in public favour throughout the eighteenth century and the early years of the nineteenth. But by the end of the nineteenth century, owing to considerable improvements in its vinification, sparkling Champagne had won the unchallenged place which it occupies today as the best of all sparkling wines.

The story of sparkling Champagne, the rôle that it has played in the commercial and social life of France, England and the United States over the past three hundred years, is what I have done my best to describe in this book. It is not my first attempt to do so. In 1904, I wrote a series of articles on the subject, at the request of one of the best friends I made when I first came to England, A. S. Gardiner: he was at the time the Editor of the *Wine Trade Review*, in which the articles appeared monthly before being published in book form, in 1905, as *The History of the Champagne Trade in England*. This book has long since been out of print, as well as out of date, and so much has happened in Champagne and to Champagne during the twentieth century, that it is high time to bring its fascinating story up to date.

The History of
Champagne

NOTE TO THE READER

The superior numbers (thus[17]) which occur in the text refer to the Bibliography at the end of the book; the superior letters (thus[a]) refer to the notes at the end of the chapter in which they occur.

CHAPTER ONE
La Champagne

L A CHAMPAGNE is the ageless and ever fruitful mother of *le Champagne*, the best known and, indeed, the best of all sparkling wines.

It was *campus*, a field, which gave birth to *campania*, an open stretch or fairly flat tract of country, and *campania* became *champaign* in French, and the name, with the finally accepted spelling *Champagne*, was given to one of the old provinces of France, east of Paris, south of Flanders, west of Lorraine and north of Burgundy, some 125 miles wide from west to east and 170 miles long from north to south. In England, there were *champaigns*, as well as woodlands and vineyards, in the days of Domesday Book. There is today, close to Cognac, a Grande Champagne and a Petite Champagne, which owe their name to their chalky subsoil not unlike that of la Champagne: the rather dull white wine of their vineyards, when distilled, produces the finest brandy in the world. But nowhere in France, or anywhere else in the world, is there land comparable to that of the old province of Champagne for the variety of its natural beauty, a quality matched by the fame of its wine and the glorious war records of its sons. There are, in Champagne, some great stretches of rather barren country east and south of Châlons-sur-Marne, where men have

Plate 2 PINOT. The noble grape of Champagne.

been trained for war since the days of Julius Caesar, but there are also rivers, large and small, wooded hills and sheep grazings, busy cities and sleepy hamlets, besides the vineyards which have been a source of pride and wealth for nearly two thousand years.

The Champagne vineyards have not the *sauvage grandeur* of those of the Alto Douro, but they are nonetheless very beautiful, spreading their emerald folds up and down the slopes of the Montagne de Reims towards Vesle or Marne, for miles and miles, as far as the eye can see, and almost swamping the squat, grey houses, huddled around their old village church, where for generations past *vignerons* have lived for and by *la Champagne*.

Here and there a clump of great trees, beacon-like on high ground, marks the site of some famous château, within its own park, the home of one or other of those old French families who, for generations past, have lived for and by *le Champagne*.

When the provinces of France were done away with, at the time of the French Revolution, they were replaced by smaller administrative divisions called *départements*. The Champagne province was divided into four of those *départements* i.e., *Marne* (Châlons-sur-Marne, Reims and Epernay); *Aube* (Troyes); *Haute-Marne* (Chaumont); and *Ardennes* (Mézières). Parts of the former Champagne province were also included in four other nearby *départements*, i.e. *Aisne* (Laon); *Yonne* (Auxerre); *Seine-et-Marne* (Château-Thierry); and *Meuse* (Bar-le-Duc). There are vineyards in all eight *départements*, a few only in some, a great many in others; but the fact that their vines are rooted in soil that was once within the boundaries of the old Champagne province does not give to their wine the right to assume the honoured name of Champagne. No wine has any right to that name other than the sparkling wine made from grapes grown in the vineyards of the strictly limited area known as the *région délimitée de la Champagne viticole*. The vineyards within the boundaries of this *région* are those where the soil and sub-soil are such that they can give to the noble Pinot grapes in major or minor measure, the minerals they must have if they are to bring forth wines possessing the inimitable characteristics of the best sparkling Champagne.

The vineyards within the *région délimitée* added up to some 27,000 acres before 1940: 21,000 acres (77.8 %) in the Marne *département*, 4,600 (17 %) in the

Aube, and 1,400 acres (5.2 %) in the Aisne. We propose, however, to ignore the vineyards of the Aube and Aisne and to deal solely with those of the Marne. In so doing, however, we are merely following the example of some of the more illustrious authorities of the nineteenth century – Chaptal,[21] Napoleon's Ministre de l'Intérieur, A. Jullien,[28] Cavoleau,[32] and others.

The present acreage of the Marne vineyards is only a little more than half what it was in 1818 when, according to the *Annuaire du département de la Marne* for 1819, there were 41,300 acres in bearing, a figure which has never ceased to shrink since then. According to the *Œnologie française*, there were 38,300 acres in 1827, and 37,000 in 1836; and according to Dr Guyot's *Viticulture de la France*, there were 35,200 acres in 1868. By 1906, after the disastrous effects of the phylloxera had largely been remedied, 30,500 acres were in cultivation; the number declined to 28,290 in 1913, and to 21,708 in 1918. During the First World War the Champagne vineyards suffered more grievously than any of the other vineyards of France.

Since then, much has been done to check further inroads of the phylloxera, and a number of the old vineyards which had gone out of cultivation have now been replanted. In 1959, the number of acres in cultivation was 25,000.[69]

The inimitable excellence of the wines produced from the vineyards of the Marne is due in the first place to the soil, in which there happens to be a very peculiar kind of chalk called *craie à hélemnites*; this is mixed with a top soil of sand, clay, leaf and manure compost, to say nothing of the sweat of man and beast. The *vignerons* dress their vineyards every year with this mixture.

Montagne de Reims

The Montagne de Reims is a bluff or cliff of cretaceous and tertiary formation in a shape somewhat like a great flat-iron, the point of which faces Châlons-sur-Marne. It rises sharply from the billowing plain west of Châlons-sur-Marne, with the little river Vesle on the north-east side and the river Marne to the south-west. A great forest – which is one of the few wild boar sanctuaries left in France – covers the broad crest of the Montagne de Reims, but its slopes and approaches are covered with closely planted vineyards on all sides. The

part of the Montagne facing Reims, and the farthest from Châlons-sur-Marne, is known as *La Petite Montagne*, and its vineyards produce much wine, most of it undistinguished although of fair enough quality in good vintages; two of the best of these are the wines of Villedommange and Sacy.

For many centuries, and up to the present day, only those wines which are made from the vineyards on the Vesle and Reims side of the Montagne de Reims have been known as *Montagne* wines, whereas the wines from the vineyards on the other side of the Montagne, facing the river Marne, have always been known as Valley or River wines.

The first quality vineyards of the Montagne de Reims, from west to east, are those of Villers-Allerand; then come those of Chigny-les-Roses, Rilly-la-Montagne, Ludes, Mailly-Champagne, Verzenay, Verzy and Villers-Marmery – all of them hillside vineyards. With the forest behind them and countless vines in serried rank before them, they stretch to Sillery and Beaumont-sur-Vesle and the *route nationale* from Reims to Châlons-sur-Marne, forming a truly wonderful panorama. When we come to the point of the "flat-iron", Trépail, Vaudemange, Tauxières, Louvois, Bouzy and Ambonnay, bring us to the Valley of the Marne.

Valley of the Marne

If we follow the right bank of the Marne, turning our backs on Châlons-sur-Marne and facing Château-Thierry and Paris further west, we shall come to the vineyards of Tours-sur-Marne, Bisseuil, Mareuil-sur-Ay, Avenay and Mutigny a little way up the hill; Ay-Champagne, Dizy-Magenta, Cumières and Damery nearer the river; Champillon and Hautvillers further up-hill.

Crossing the Marne at Epernay, the nearest vineyards on the left bank of the river are those of Oiry, Chouilly and Pierry; then, a little farther back, we come to the Côte des Blancs – to Cuis, Cramant, Avize, Oger, Le Mesnil-sur-Oger, and Vertus, all upon slopes facing – at a distance – the Marne. Upon the other side of the Côte des Blancs range of hills, there are more vineyards, none of them, however, in the very top rank: the best of them are those of Grauves and Monthelon.

The *catégorie* to which each of the many Champagne vineyards belongs is of very great importance to the *vignerons*, as the price which they get from the shippers at vintage time depends upon it.

Just as the vintage is about to begin each year, the delegates of the growers' and merchants' syndicates meet to discuss what will be the price of the grapes of the *Hors Classe Catégorie*. It is on the agreed scale of percentages of this price that the prices of the grapes of the other *catégories* are based as follows:

> 90 % to 98 % for grapes of the *Première Catégorie*
> 80 % to 88 % for those of *Deuxième Catégorie*
> 70 % to 78 % for those of the *Troisième Catégorie*
> 60 % to 68 % for those of the *Quatrième Catégorie*
> 50 % to 58 % for those of the *Cinquième Catégorie*

The flexibility of price in each case allows for the varying standard of quality to be found among the grapes of the different vineyards within each *catégorie*.

There are, in the Marne *département*, one hundred and fifty-five villages, the vineyards of which are responsible for producing nearly 78 % of all the wines entitled to the name of Champagne. There are great differences in the quality of their wines, however, and not more than twelve of these villages belong to the *Hors Classe* (or 100 %) *Catégorie*. There are eight other villages which produce very fine grapes, though they are not quite equal to those of the first twelve; their grapes will be paid for at the rate of from 90 % to 98 % of the price agreed to for the first. The grapes of twenty-four villages are graded from 80 % to 88 % of the "100 %" price, those of forty-seven villages are graded from 70 % to 78 %, and those of sixty-four villages are graded from 50 % to 68 %.

Unlike Claret, Burgundy, Hock, Moselle and many other beverage wines, Champagne is not the wine of any individual vineyard but a blend of wines from a number of Champagne vineyards, and it is obvious that if the greater proportion of wines in a blend come from the 80 % to 100 % vineyards, the better, and also the more expensive, the wine will be.

Here is a list of the better Champagne vineyards of the first three *catégories*; figures indicate acreage:

HORS CLASSE 100%

Canton de Verzy

Beaumont-sur-Vesle	95	Sillery	277
Mailly	262	Verzenay	750
Puisieulx	20		

Canton d'Ay

Ambonnay	450	Louvois	62
Ay-Champagne	1,000	Tours-sur-Marne*	37
Bouzy	477		

Canton d'Avize

Avize	487	Cramant	640

PREMIÈRE CATÉGORIE 90% — 98%

Canton de Reims

Murigny	95

Canton de Verzy

Verzy	575

Canton d'Ay

Dizy-Magenta	352	Tauxières	75
Mareuil-sur-Ay	647		

Canton d'Avize

Le Mesnil-sur-Oger	700	Oiry	225
Oger	550		

* Black grapes only

DEUXIÈME CATÉGORIE 80% — 88%

Canton de Verzy

Chigny-les-Roses	250	Trépail	325
Ludes	425	Villers-Allerand	65
Rilly-la-Montagne	675	Villers-Marmery	407
Avenay	450	Hautvillers	650
Bisseuil	22	Mutigny	300
Champillon	137	Vaudemange	67
Cumières	442		

Canton d'Avize

Cuis	1,000	Grauves	250

Canton de Vertus

Bergères-les-Vertus	322	Vertus	1,127

Canton d'Epernay

Chouilly	615	Pierry	262

Canton de Ville-en-Tardenois

Ecueil	215	Sacy	212
Les Mesneux	17	Villedommange	299

An Alphabetical List of the Wine-producing Villages of the Marne Département with their Grading

Ambonnay	100	Beaunay	70
Avenay	86	Belval-sous-Chatillon	62
Avize	100	Bergères-les-Vertus	86
Ay-Champagne	100	Binson-Orquigny	66
Baslieux	62	Bisseuil	80
Baye	70	Bligny	62
Beaumont-sur-Veslè	100	Bouilly	72

Boursault	60	Damery	72
Bouzy	100	Dizy	90
Branscourt	68	Dormans	62
Brouillet	70	Ecueil	80
Brugny-Vaudancourt	72	Epernay	76
Cauroy	62	Etoges	70
Chambrecy	58	Faverolles	72
Chamery	76	Férebrianges	70
Champillon	86	Festigny	62
Champlat-Boujacourt	62	Fleury-la-Rivière	66
Champvoisy	64	Germigny	70
Chassins	64	Givry-les-Loizy	70
Châtillon-sur-Marne	64	Grauves	86
Chaumuzy	60	Gueux	70
Chavot-Courcourt	76	Hautvillers	80
Chenay	64	Hermonville	64
Chigny-les-Roses	88	Hourges	72
Chouilly	86	Janvry	68
Coizard-Joches	70	Jonquery	66
Coligny	70	Jouy	78
Comblizy	60	Lagery	70
Congy	70	La-Neuville-aux-Larris	62
Cormicy	70	Le Breuil	62
Cormoyeux	66	Le Mesnil-sur-Oger	98
Coulommes-la-Montagne	78	Le Mesnil-Hutier	64
Courjeonnet	70	Les Mesneux	80
Courmas	72	Leuvrigny	64
Courthiezy	62	Lhéry	70
Cramant	100	Loisy-en-Brie	70
Crugny	72	Louvois	100
Cuchery	60	Ludes	88
Cuis	80	Mailly	100
Cuisles	63	Mancy	76
Cumières	80	Mardeuil	64

Mareuil-le-Port	64	Saint-Thierry	74
Mareuil-sur-Ay	95	Sarcy	62
Marfaux	62	Savigny-sur-Ardre	74
Merfy	64	Sermières	76
Montholon	76	Sercy-et-Prin	72
Montigny-sous-Châtillon	66	Sillery	100
Morangis	68	Soilly	62
Moussy	76	Soulières	70
Murigny	92	Talus-St-Prix	70
Mutigny		Tauxières	90
Nesle-le-Repons	60	Thil	64
Nogent-l'Abesse	70	Toulon-la-Montagne	70
Œuilly	62	Tours-sur-Marne	100
Oger	98	Tramery	70
Oiry	98	Tréloup	64
Oizy-Violaine	64	Trépail	80
Pargny	78	Treslong	72
Passy-Grigny	64	Trigny	60
Passy-sur-Marne	64	Troissy-Bouquigny	62
Pevy	62	Unchair	72
Pierry	80	Vauciennes	60
Poilly	62	Vaudemange	80
Pouillon	64	Vaudeuil	72
Pourcy	64	Vaudières	64
Provilly	64	Venteuil	70
Puisieulx	100	Verneuil	64
Reuil	64	Vert-la-Grevelle	64
Rilly-la-Montagne	88	Vertus	86
Romery	66	Verzenay	100
Rosnay	62	Verzy	98
Sacy	80	Villedommange	80
Sainte-Euphrasie	42	Ville-en-Tardenois	58
Sainte-Gemme	64	Villevenard	70
Saint-Martin d'Ablois	72	Villers-Allerand	80

Villers-Franqueux	64	Vinay	72
Villers-Marmery	80	Vincelles	66
Villers-sous-Châtillon	66	Vrigny	78

The average production of the vineyards in the 100 % class is 1,899,781 gallons, or 24.5 % of the total production of the first five classes; the production of the vineyards with the 90 % to 98 % grading is 830,161 gallons, or 11.5 % of the total; the vineyards with the 80 % to 88 % grading average 1,861,314 gallons, or 24 %; those with the 70 % to 78 % grading average 1,426,682 gallons, or 19.5 %; and those with a 60 % to 68 % grading average 1,630,288 gallons, or 20.5 %.[63]

The great majority of the 14,000 *vignerons* of the Marne own less than 5 acres of vines, many of them less than 1 acre, and they all would like, naturally, to get top prices for their grapes if they could. But there is nothing they can do about having their holding raised from a lower to a higher *catégorie*, since the rating of all Champagne vineyards depends in the first place upon the geological formation of the soil; also, to a lesser but by no means negligible degree, to their aspect, elevation and gradient.

In 1929, when there were 11,298 vignerons in the Marne *département*, their holdings were as follows:

4,300 owned less than 1 acre each
4,770 owned more than 1 acre and less than 2½ acres
2,080 owned more than 2½ acres and less than 12½ acres
87 owned more than 12½ acres and less than 25 acres
38 owned more than 25 acres and less than 50 acres
18 owned more than 50 acres and less than 125 acres
5 owned more than 125 acres

The Grapes

The nature of the soil has, of course, a great deal to do with the excellence and distinctive characteristics of Champagne, but the grapes from which the wine is made are also of paramount importance. All the best wines made in Champagne are Pinot wines, some 80 % of them black Pinots, of which there are different varieties. The best, or at any rate the one which is grown to a greater extent than all others, is the one known locally as *Plant Doré*. There are now three slightly different sorts of this noble grape, one called *Le Petit Plant Doré*, another *Le Gros Plant Doré d'Ay*, and a third known indifferently as *Le Vert Doré* or *Plant Jeanson* or *Plant d'Ay*. Other varieties of black Pinots – which, incidentally, are not black but midnight blue – are the *Plant Gris*, which must not be mistaken for the *Pinot Gris*, a white variety; the *Pinot de Trépail* and the *Pinot de Vertus*. All these are "noble" Pinots, but they have a poor relation, *Le Pinot Meunier*, a more generous but commoner species, giving more gallons per acre of a less distinguished wine.

The white grapes of Champagne are practically all Chardonnay grapes and the vines which bear them are called either *Pinot Chardonnay*, *Blanc de Cramant* or *Pinot Blanc Chardonnay*.

CHAPTER TWO

Le Champagne

L<small>E</small> CHAMPAGNE is the sparkling wine made from Pinot grapes grown within the boundaries of the *Champagne viticole*, the legally defined area of the Champagne vineyards. It owes its characteristic qualities to the Pinot grapes and to the peculiar geological formation of the soil and sub-soil of the vineyards; and also to the *méthode champenoise*, that is to say, to the way in which the wine is handled from the vintage time, when the grapes are pressed, until it is ready to be sold and drunk, perhaps four or five, or even ten or more years later.

Sparkling Champagne is a white wine; it can also be made pink, and the little of it that is made pink is called *rosé*. Most white wines are made from white grapes, but white Champagne is made mostly from grapes which we call black, although their skins are blue outside and red inside. Their juice, however, is white, and it will make white wine provided it is not allowed to be coloured by the pigment in the red lining of the skin of ripe black grapes. So, at the time of the vintage, the grapes are picked with care and brought to the *pressoir*, without being bruised, but after having been *épluchés* – that is, examined at the roadside, near the vineyard of their birth, by a team of women, most of them elderly, who have had their full share of the back-breaking work of grape picking when they were younger. They sit in a row with a wide osier tray at knee height before them; the grapes which have been gathered are brought to these women by the pickers in baskets which are tipped over on to the osier trays. The women quickly take up and look over each bunch, removing expertly, with a pair of long pointed scissors, any defective berries – those that are unripe, mildewed, bird- or insect-pecked, etc. All such "rejects" are dropped into a refuse bin, while the bunches with none but sound and ripe grapes go into great osier baskets called *caques*. These are loaded on to lorries and driven to the nearest *vendangeoir* of the shipper concerned, who either owns the vineyard or has bought the grapes from their owner. At the *vendangeoir*, the grapes are weighed in their *caques* and tipped into the *pressoir*, until there is enough for one pressing or *charge* – usually 4,000 kg., or nearly 4 tons.

The *pressoir* consists of a square wooden floor with four adjustable open-work wooden rails which make a sort of cage in which the grapes are heaped. There is a heavy lid of oak boards which is lowered and raised at will by a screw, driven formerly by sweat and muscle, but nowadays by pressing a button. When this heavy lid is clamped on the heaped grapes and slowly but relentlessly driven down, its crushing pressure bursts the grapes, so that their sweet juice soon starts running through the rails into a slightly sloping groove. This groove leads to a collecting "station", where the juice arrives without having been in contact with the red dye of the grape-skins, which are left in the cage of the *pressoir*. The first flow of the grape-juice is either run or pumped into a vat which holds 450 gallons: it will make the best wine and it is called the *cuvée*. Greater pressure is then applied and more juice is squeezed out of the wet husks still in the cage of the *pressoir*, but this juice is not as white, nor as sweet, nor as good as that from the first pressing: it is not mixed with it.

Soon after the grape-juice has been lodged in its fermenting vat, it starts fermenting of its own accord and in a somewhat boisterous fashion, throwing off an ugly "head" or scum: this is its way of getting rid of dust, dirt and anything that is unwanted other than the heavier "discards" which fall to the bottom of the vat and form the lees. When the "must", as this fermenting grape-juice is called, returns to a more normal temperature (in approximately 24 or 36 hours as a rule), all the clear liquid in the vat has to be removed for storage. At one time, the liquid was drawn into clean oak casks holding 44 gallons each, and the casks were then immediately sent by lorries to the cellars of the firm owning the wine; nowadays, however, tanks on wheels, similar to those used for petrol or milk, are replacing the old-fashioned oak casks for transport, and glass-lined steel tanks are used for storing the "must" and the new wine.

The "must" is now left alone, and after a period of between eight to ten weeks, during which fermentation takes place at an increasingly slower rate, it becomes "new wine". The new wines are then "racked", that is, run from their original casks or tanks into fresh ones, leaving behind the sediment formed and cast off in the fermentation process. Then all the wines made from the grapes of the same vineyard in the course of the vintage are "assembled" or blended together; this ensures that the wines of each particular vineyard will be exactly alike, whether the grapes were picked at the beginning or at the end of the *vendange*.

The wines are given another few weeks of rest before being "racked" again, which serves the double purpose of taking them away from any lees or sediment they may have cast off again, and letting in a free supply of oxygen, which helps the final stages of fermentation. Then comes the all-important business of making up the *cuvées*. The *Chef de caves*, whose responsibility it is, must taste with the greatest precision the wines of the different vineyards in the firm's *celliers*, and he has to decide how much or how little of the wines of each different district he should blend together, to arrive at the right quantity and quality of each of the different *cuvées* which his firm will eventually offer for sale in different parts of the world, in competition with the wines of other Champagne shippers.

The making of each Champagne shipper's *cuvées* is the jealously guarded secret of the *Chef de caves*, but there is good cause to believe that the selection made over a hundred years ago by a Reims *Chef de caves*, as recorded in *Wine, the Vine and the Cellar*, by Thomas George Shaw (published London, 1863), is not essentially different from the kind of selection which goes into the making of a good *cuvée* today:

Black grape wines

Verzenay	5 hogsheads
Bouzy	5
Chigny	2½
Ay	5
Champillon	2½
Pierry	5
Vertus	5
	30 hogsheads

White grape wines

Cramant and Avize	10 hogsheads
Le Mesnil	5
Chouilly	2½
Crayons de St-Martin	2½
	20 hogsheads

It is also for the *Chef de caves* to decide how much any of the older wines which are always kept in reserve for the purpose should be blended with the new wine. When, after many tastings, comparisons, hesitations and discussions with his staff, the *Chef de caves* makes his final decision, the chosen wines are thoroughly well blended in great *foudres* or vats, a mechanical arm – electrically actioned – churning up the whole contents of each *foudre*. The wine is now ready for bottling. A careful testing is carried out to ascertain exactly how much grape-sugar, if any, is still present. The *liqueur de tirage* is then added accordingly; it is made up of sugar melted in white Champagne wine and the quantity of it that is added to the wine immediately before it is bottled is exactly calculated to produce, by a second fermentation of the wine in the bottle, the right amount of carbonic acid gas – not too much, in case the gas bursts the bottles, nor too little, in case too few bubbles show up and the wine is flat.

The freshly sugared new wine is then bottled and safely corked with a plastic cork, which is held by a "crown" cork – this will keep it in place at the *prise de mousse*, when the *liqueur de tirage* has done its work and the fermentation has produced a sufficient amount of carbonic acid gas to make the wine sparkling.

The fermentation also produces a certain amount of sediment, though this would not spoil the look or taste of the wine so long as it was left at peace on the inside face of the bottle; it would inevitably mix with the wine, however, once the cork had been removed and the wine poured out. So all sediment has to be removed completely before the wine can be offered for sale. This is done very skilfully by what is called *remuage* and *dégorgement*. The remuage consists in giving each bottle, week after week, a twist sharp enough to make the sediment slide along towards the neck of the bottle, but not hard enough to make it rise into the wine. The *remueur* begins his work on bottles which lie almost horizontally in two *pupitres*, specially constructed tables made in pairs hinged at the top so that they can stand firmly in an upright position, and set about four feet apart on the ground. Each time the *remueur* gives a bottle a firm yet gentle shake, he has to lift it just a little off its table socket and, when replacing it, he lifts the punt of the bottle very slightly and pushes the neck just a little further into the table socket. When he has been doing this for some weeks – according to the nature of the sediment inside, which may be more or less difficult to move – the bottle will be standing vertically, cork down and punt up. By then all the sediment will have collected on the inside face of the cork.

The next step is to remove the cork, together with its little wad of dirt or sediment, leaving the wine in the bottle absolutely "star" bright. This must be done, and it is done, with practically no loss of wine or gas. The man who does this is called the *dégorgeur*, and he is a skilled and valuable man indeed. His task is now much easier than it used to be owing to the practice now in use of dipping the neck of the bottle in a refrigerating bath, out of which it comes with about one inch of the wine just below the cork completely frozen and containing all the collected sediment.

The *dégorgeur* is the first of a *chantier*, or team, who deal with each bottle of Champagne when the time has come for it to leave the depths of the cellars for the outside world, where its sparkling and joyful message is thirstily awaited. After the *dégorgeur* comes the man whose job it is to add to each bottle whatever quantity of *liqueur d'expédition* it should have: this is a very sticky mixture of sugar melted in white wine – Champagne wine, of course – and a small amount of very pale and very fine brandy, the function of which is to ensure that the added sugar does not start fermenting later on. Although Champagne which is absolutely *brut* or *nature* should not, in principle, contain any addition of *liqueur d'expédition*, it is in fact a fairly general practice to add from ¼ % to 1½ %; if sold as Extra Dry, Extra Sec or Très Sec, the Champagne may have from 1½ % to 2 % of *liqueur d'expédition* added, whereas the Dry or Sec Champagnes may have from 2½ % to 5 %; the Demi-sec from 5 % to 8 %; and the Doux from 8 % to 12 %. Most Champagne prepared for the French market is sweeter than the majority of export Champagne, but there was a time, before the Russian Revolution, when incredibly sweet Champagne – sometimes with an addition of 20 % of *liqueur d'expédition* – was sold in Russia, and they used to say at the time that Grand Dukes liked their Champagne laced with Yellow Chartreuse.

Liqueur d'expédition is not a standardised product: each firm makes its own *liqueur d'expédition* as it thinks best, so that some *liqueurs* are actually sweeter than others; hence the Champagne shipped by "A" with a 1 % addition of *liqueur* may be as sweet or rather as dry as the Champagne shipped by "B" with an addition of 1¼ %. [10]

Next to the *doseur* sits the *chef de chantier* who is also the *boucheur* responsible

Rue du Mail, n° 9, près les Petits Pères.

VENTE DE VINS FINS,
ET BON ORDINAIRE.
A PRIX FIXE.

Passage Choiseul, n. 80, sous l'Horloge.

NORMAND, MARCHAND DE VINS,

Tient et reçoit un entrepôt des vins de toutes qualités, en pièces et en bouteilles, pour être exposés à la vente et à la dégustation, à prix fixe, annoncé par une étiquette sur chaque espèce de vin; il fait des avances sur les marchandises qui lui sont consignées; procure une vente prompte aux Marchands, et de bons marchés aux Consommateurs, qui sont invités à venir avec toute confiance visiter ses caves et magasins, tant ceux de son nouvel établissement, *Passage Choiseul*, que ceux qu'il tient depuis nombre d'années, *rue du Mail*, n° 9, et qui fournissent à la consommation des premières Maisons de la Capitale qui ont reconnu qu'il y avait un grand avantage à n'avoir pas de vins fins en cave, tant par la facilité d'avoir un compte exact de la consommation, que pour leur conservation, qui exige une grande attention.

Nota. On trouve à l'établissement du Passage Choiseul, un salon, où l'on donne en consommation les vins fins du magasin, depuis 2 francs la bouteille jusqu'aux plus hauts prix cotés ci-après.

Prix-Courant.

Vins de Bourgogne.

ROUGE.

	fr.	c.
Clos-Vougeot	5	»
Chambertin	4	»
Volnay	3	»
Nuits	2	50
Beaune, 1re qualité	2	»
Beaune, 2e qualité	1	25
Coulanges	1	25
Pomard	3	50

BLANC.

	fr.	c.
Montrachet	3	»
Meursault	2	»
Chablis, 1re qualité	1	25
Chablis, 2e qualité	1	»
Bourgogne mousseux	5	»

Vins de Mâcon.

ROUGE.

	fr.	c.
Moulin à vent	2	»
Thorins	1	50
Mâcon, 1re qualité	1	25
Mâcon, 2e qualité	1	»

Vins de Champagne.

	fr.	c.
Sillery	5	»
Champagne Aï	4	50
Champagne Aï rosé	4	50
Champagne Epernay	3	50
Champagne Epernay rosé	3	50
Tisanne	2	»

Vins de Bordeaux.

ROUGE.

	fr.	c.
Bordeaux ordinaire	»	60
Bordeaux-Laffite	6	»
Château-Margaux	4	»
Saint-Julien, 1re qualité	3	»
Saint-Julien, 2e qualité	2	»
Saint-Estèphe	2	50
Saint-Émilion	1	50

BLANC.

	fr.	c.
Barsac	3	»
Sauterne	4	»
Graves	2	»

Vins du Rhône et du Midi.

ROUGE.

	fr.	c.
Saint-Georges	2	50
Côte-Rôtie	2	»
Tavel	1	50
Roussillon	1	50
Hermitage	3	50

BLANC.

	fr.	c.
Blanquette de Limoux	3	»
Saint-Perray	3	»
Hermitage	4	»

Vins d'Orléans.

ROUGE.

	fr.	c.
Beaugency	1	»
Orléans	»	60

Vins de Liqueurs.

	fr.	c.
Vins du Rhin	10	»
Muscat de Frontignan	2	50
Muscat de Lunel	3	»
Grenache	2	50
Malaga	4	»
Alicante	3	50
Madère	3	»
Porto	4	50

Eaux-de-vie et Liqueurs.

	fr.	c.
Rhum	2	50
Kirchenwasser	3	50
Eau-de-vie de Cognac	2	25
Eau-de-vie de Montpellier	1	25
Huile de vanille	3	»
Huile de rose	2	50
Crême de menthe	2	50
Crême de fleur d'orange	2	50
Curaçao de Hollande	2	50
Anisette de Bordeaux	2	50
Scubac de Lorraine	3	»
Absinthe	2	50
Eau de fleur d'orange double.		

On vend de l'Eau-de-vie et de l'Esprit 3/6 à la velte. On trouve en pièces, au prix le plus juste, la plupart des vins désignés ci-dessus.

Il garantit l'origine des Vins, telle qu'elle est annoncée par l'étiquette, et sans aucune altération.

Paris, le 18 *[manuscrit]*

Vendu à M. *[manuscrit]*

for driving into the neck of the bottle the cork branded with the name of the firm, and, in the case of vintage *cuvées*, the date of the wine's vintage.

For the bottle or "reputed" quart, the corks are about 2 in. long (from 48 to 55 millimetres); their diameter is 1.2 in. (32½ millimetres) which is exactly double that of the diameter of the bottle neck. The *boucheur* has first of all to squeeze the cork to half its original size, and then drive one inch of it – i.e. half its length – into the neck of the bottle.

Next to the *boucheur* sits the *ficeleur* who crushes down the half of the cork jutting out of the neck of the bottle and makes it fast below the ring of the bottle-neck with specially made cap and wire. The bottle then gets a vigorous shaking from a lad, the last member of the *chantier*, who stands up (like the *dégorgeur* at the other end), his job being to ensure that the *liqueur d'expédition* added to the wine by the *doseur* is thoroughly well mixed with the wine.

All there is now left to do is to bin away the liqueured and finally corked bottles until the call comes for them to be sent up to the packing rooms, there to be washed, labelled, wrapped up and packed in cartons, hampers or cases, and then to be sent to whatever part of the world from which the demand has come.

Up till now no machine has been perfected that can do the work of the *dégorgeur*, but all the *dégorgeur's* mates can be, and indeed in some firms already have been, replaced by wonderful machines!

The day may come when there will be no longer any *pupitres*, *remueurs* or *dégorgeurs* in Champagne cellars and when Champagne will be made as Sekt is being made today by one of the most progressive German firms of the Rhineland, by filtering the wine which contains the sediment. They claim that it is a more hygienic technique since the wine is at no time in contact with a human hand.

Champagne rosé. It may be as well to make it plain here that pink Champagne is not dyed with cochineal, elderberry juice or anything else; nor is it made only in exceptionally hot years from overripe grapes: it is made simply by adding to any white wine of Champagne the right quantity of red wine of Champagne, mostly wine of Bouzy, occasionally wine of Ambonnay or Trépail, to give it the right degree of colour. This is done, of course, before the bottling of the wine, and it sometimes happens that during the secondary fermentation in bottle, the wine loses more of its colour than had been expected; in such a case, the *doseur*, as soon as the bottle has been *dégorgée*, adds a *correctif* dose of red wine to get the right shade of *rosé* colour.

Blanc de Blancs. Several Champagne shippers sell, under the name of *Blanc de Blancs, cuvées* made up entirely of Pinot Chardonnay grapes, a white wine (*Blanc*) of white grapes (*de Blancs*). Such a wine is always very pale in colour, and it is usually also lighter in body, but not necessarily in alcoholic strength, than the majority of other *cuvées* which are blends of white wines from both black grapes and white grapes. Dry and elegant, it is an ideal wine to serve before a meal, or as the first wine of the day in the forenoon after a late night.

The Service of Champagne. Champagne should be served cold, as everybody knows – yet not everybody has the same notion of *how* cold.

The coldest bottle of Champagne I ever saw, though I did not drink it, was at the Plaza Hotel in Buenos Aires in 1908: I had ordered in the morning our dinner for the evening, and a bottle of Pommery, which they must have put into an ice-box immediately. The waiter managed to get the cork out, very quietly, without a "pop"; but when he tried to serve the wine, not a drop came out! The wine in the neck of the bottle was frozen solid . . . When finally served, the wine was frost-bitten and quite undrinkable.

The ideal temperature for Champagne is the temperature of those great Reims *crayères* or chalk pits used as cellars, some 100 feet deep, which very rarely rises above 10½° Centigrade (50° Fahrenheit); but a bottle of Champagne taken from a bin under the stairs, or from its straw envelope still in its original case, must not be chilled too quickly nor too much. It should be left to cool for an hour or so in ice-cold water and no longer. If packed in crushed ice and left too long, the wine will suffer from shock; it will be too cold and quite "dumb". Too sweet, too cold or too much Champagne is a mistake: its reward is a sore head and an unholy thirst the morning after.

When the wire muzzle which holds the cork has been released, the bottle should be held in a slanting position; the cork must be held firmly and eased slowly until it leaves the neck of the bottle, with as little noise as possible. If the gas in solution in the wine is given the chance, it will send the cork flying to the ceiling with a loud report, and a flood of bubbling wine will rush out and be lost.

Before serving Champagne, it is wise to smell critically the first glass, and make sure that the wine is absolutely "clean", that is, free from any corkiness or mouldiness. Every bottle of Champagne is at the mercy of its cork, and there is no way of being certain that each cork will behave as it ought to. Just a few will turn mouldy and ruin the wine which they were meant to protect.

Swizzles or Mossers. These are horrible modern gadgets which ruin Champagne. There are barbarians who use a fork to do the same evil work. This is not merely the opinion of an old man who cannot help being old-fashioned; it is shared by a young American author, Alexis Lichine, who writes:

> Everyone who loves Champagne is shocked by the current ridiculous fad for swizzle sticks, those abominations which allow the uncomprehending to twirl all the bubbles out of the sparkling wine. Some even go as far as to have their own special swizzles made out of platinum and gold always ready for instant use in the fashionable bars and night clubs of Paris and Rome, London and New York. With a few twirls of the swizzle, years of special care and labour can be destroyed in seconds.[65]

There are people, of course, with either weak or defective diaphragms, or who are otherwise allergic to sparkling wines, and the best thing they can and should do is to leave Champagne alone.

CHAPTER THREE

Before Dom Pérignon

THE MARNE DÉPARTEMENT MAY RIGHTLY be called the heart of the old Champagne province, a heart that has throbbed with wine for close upon two thousand years, that is, since the Roman occupation. Pliny (A.D. 23-79) records that the wine of Reims was one of those which were fit for a royal table. But the Romans did more than introduce the culture of the vine and the art of making wine in the Valley of the Marne. They quarried for chalk on the outskirts of Reims, to make their wonderful roads, so well and for so long that they left us those great *crayères* or chalk pits, from 200 to 300 feet deep, where millions upon millions of bottles of Champagne have since found an ideal temporary home, absolutely safe from all changes of temperature in the coldest of winters and the hottest of summers.

A very, very long time before there were any Romans and Gauls, before there were any thirsty men at all, there were vines not far from Epernay, at Sézanne, where Dr Lemoine and M. Balbiani found fossils of the *Vitis rotundifolia* which have been named *Vitis sezannensis* and *Vitis balbianii*.[55]

The fact that grapes would grow and bring forth good wine when planted upon any of the slopes of the hills between Marne and Vesle, or Reims and

Epernay, was duly appreciated by the Church, and when St Rémi, first Archbishop of Reims, died in A.D. 530, vineyards were among the more important
of his bequests. In A.D. 743, when King Dagobert died, he bequeathed to the
clergy of Reims his vineyards of Fleury-la-Rivière and Taissy. There are still
some vineyards at Fleury-la-Rivière but none at Taissy. In the 1848 edition
of Jullien's *Topographie de tous les vignobles connus* (p. 42) the red wines of Taissy
are given as the peers of those Sillery, Ludes, Chigny, Rilly and Villers-
Allerand.

In or about A.D. 1200, Henri d'Andelys, in his *Bataille des Vins*, names the
wines of Epernay, Reims and Hautvillers among the best wines from all the
vinelands of Europe competing for a prize of excellence before Philippe-
Auguste.[27]

The Montagne de Reims vineyards and those of the Marne are rich in lime,
which is far more precious than gold, since it remains whereas gold soon
vanishes. They have brought forth wines all through the centuries for the
greater good of the privileged few among princely, royal, imperial and ponti-
fical lovers of fine wine. Thus Urban II (1088-99), speaking privately and as a
Champenois by birth, declared that there never was a better wine than the
wine of Ay. [18] One of his successors, Pope Leo X (1513-21) had, according to
tradition, a vineyard of his own in Champagne; there is a strip of vines on the
right of the road from Damery to Ay which is known to this day as *Le Léon*,
and, according to local tradition, it is part of the original vineyard of Pope
Leo X.[36] It has also been often said and written, although so far without the
support of any documentary evidence, that the three greatest monarchs of the
sixteenth century, Charles V of Spain, François Ier of France, and Henry VIII
of England, all had their own agent or broker at Ay, whose duty it was to
secure some of the best Champagne available at the time of the vintage for
their royal masters. As far as we know, there is but one record of Champagne
sent to England in the reign of Henry VIII, a letter from the French Admiral
Bonnivet, who wrote, in 1518, to Wolsey advising him that there were 20
Poinçons de Vin d'Ay on their way to him.[1]

From records of François Ier in Champagne, he was presented with some Ay
wine in 1535, when he visited Châlons-sur-Marne,[2] and, in June 1537, some
Vin d'Ay was bought for him, "as the king wished to have a sufficiency of this

wine at Compiègne and other royal residences where he expected the dowager queen of Hungary to stay during her visit to France." [3]

Good as the wines of Ay certainly were at the time, and far famed as they were, the *vignerons* of Champagne had very little chance, if any, to sell their wines to any large or commercial extent outside their great landlocked province. All their immediate neighbours had vineyards of their own, and they made wine which was quite good enough for themselves, wine which they most likely considered better than any that Champagne had to offer. Thus Parisians, whether they wished it or not, were obliged to drink either the wines of Paris vineyards or some of the *vins françoys*, at a time when *vins françoys* meant not French wines but wines from the Ile-de-France. The Ile-de-France was an island surrounded not by the sea but by the waters of five rivers, the Seine, the Marne, the Oise, the Aisne and the Ourcq: at the time of the French Revolution it was divided into the *départements* of Seine, Seine-et-Marne, Seine-et-Oise, and parts of Oise. The vineyards nearest to Paris named in a *Traicté particulier pour les vendanges des environs de Paris*, published in 1593, were: Auteuil, Bagneux, Bagnolet, Boulogne, Bourg-la-Reine, Charonne, Chastenay, Chatillon, Clamart, Clichy-la-Garenne, Clignancourt, Courcelles, Fleury, Fontenay, Ivry, La Villette, Lay, Meudon, Montmartre, Montreux, Noisy-le-Sec, Nogent, Pantin, Passy, Pré-St-Gervais, Romainville, Rosny, Sèvres, Surène, Thiers, Villejuif, Vincennes, Vitry. Internal taxes, transport difficulties and vested interests were chiefly responsible for keeping out of Paris the wines of other French vineyards and those from foreign vinelands until the first half of the seventeenth century, when Champagne first became fashionable at Court. Its position was soon challenged by Burgundy but Bordeaux did not appear till fully fifty years later.

In 1705, a Beaune doctor named Sieur de Salins Aîné published a letter which he had written to the *Conseiller du Parlement* at Dijon: in it he stated that Champagne had not been heard of in Paris before 1648, when it was introduced by Le Tellier and Colbert who had large vineyards at Reims. The doctor was wrong on two counts: the two Champenois whom he names never had vineyards at Reims. Le Tellier was Louis XIII's war minister and the father of Louvois, Louis XIV's war minister; his ancestral home was at Louvois and he probably had vineyards at nearby Bouzy, and maybe at Avenay further

away, but certainly not at or near Reims. Colbert, Louis XIV's finance minister, was born at Reims, where his father was a rich merchant who dealt
in wine and in cloth; there is no record that either father or son ever owned
any vineyards. And of course Champagne had been known in Paris a long time
before 1648.

In 1583, Charles Estienne and his son-in-law Jean Liébault named the Vin
d'Ay with those of Argenteuil, Meudon and Sèvres as among the "pleasant and
generous" wines one could expect from hillside vineyards.[4]

In his *De Vino et Pomaceo*, published in Paris in 1588, Julien de Paulmier,
a Normandy doctor, after naming a number of French wines, gives the prize
to the wine of Ay and second place to the wine of Irancy in the Yonne. He

describes the wine of Ay as very light in colour, delicious, *"subtil"*, pleasing to drink, easily digested and quickly through, adding that "this is why kings and princes often make it their favourite tipple". [5]

The first king of France who introduced Champagne at Court and who did much to make it better known beyond the frontiers of France was Henri IV, the good king of the *poule au pot du dimanche*: although he came from Béarn, by the far away Pyrénées, and although he was not crowned at Reims like most of the other kings of France, Champagne was his favourite wine. Whether he first tasted Champagne at Damery, where he had his headquarters, in 1592, during the siege of Epernay, we cannot tell, but at Ay they still show the house where Henri IV had his *vendangeoir*. According to Dom Chastelain, a Benedictine monk and a native of Reims (1702-1782), [15] the king, who was dining with Sully, his finance minister, liked the wine that his host gave him so much that he exclaimed: *"Ventre Saint Gris!* This is a finer wine than my own Ay or any other that I know. You must tell me what it is!" Of course, it was another Champagne wine, a Taissy wine, Sully called it. According to Jullien's *Topographie de tous les vignobles connus*, Taissy produced red wines of the *deuxième catégorie* in 1816. No grapes grow at Taissy now; it is but a very small village near Ludes. It may very well be, however, that Sully's friend, who had sent him the wine, lived at Taissy, and that the wine itself had been made from Mailly grapes just as all the wine that the Marquis de Sillery made from his Sillery and his Verzenay grapes was always known uniformly as "Sillery".

It is quite possible, even probable, that the close friendship of Henri IV and Bruslart de Sillery, his Ambassador at large and Chancellor, may have contributed to the king's predilection for the wines of Champagne, and also to the greater demand for them at the beginning of the seventeenth century.

What may be called the export trade of Champagne dates from that time and it was then that the Champenois succeeded for the first time in challenging the monopoly enjoyed hitherto by the Burgundians in Flanders and the Low Countries. Champagne had the geographical advantage of being nearer than Burgundy, a very real advantage at a time when the transport of so popular and so perishable a commodity as wine was both risky and costly. There was, of course, no question of any sparkling wines at the time. The wines of Champagne were, like those of Burgundy, red table wines, maybe a little lighter in colour and body but not so very much different. They were cheaper and this was a great asset, so much so that they were allowed into what today we call Benelux – Belgium, Netherlands, Luxembourg – then under Spanish rule, even when France and Spain were at war, that is, when the Champenois were not only aliens but enemy aliens. Thus, in 1642, the Champenois were allowed by the Spanish authorities the right to bring wines of the 1641 vintage to a number of named frontier places, there to be handed to subjects of Spain or neutrals who would attend to their sale. The places mentioned were Cambrai, Valenciennes, Avesnes, Philippeville, Marienbourg, Thionville, Montmédy and Givet.[9]

Somewhat unexpected evidence of the resentment which the Burgundians must have felt at the rising competition of Champagne both at Court and abroad is supplied by the thesis which one of their champions, Daniel Arbinet, published in Paris in 1652: in this, he proved to his own satisfaction that the wine of Beaune, i.e. Burgundy, was the most delightful as well as the most wholesome wine. *Ergo vinum belnense potuum est suavissimum, ita et saluberrimum.* The challenge was, of course, taken up by the Champenois and thus began a pen war,[36] in prose and in verse and conducted mostly in Latin, in which doctors and poets sang the praises of either Champagne or Burgundy. The war lasted for over a century. In a *Recueil de poésies latines et françoyses sur les vins de Champagne et de Bourgogne*, published in Paris in 1721, Charles Caffin's Latin ode *Campania vindicata* is given with a French translation by M. de Bellechaume: *La Champagne vangée* [sic] *ou la louange du Vin de Champagne*. In 1825 the same ode was translated anew into French by the Comte Louis de Chevigné, the son-in-law of the famous Madame Veuve Clicquot-Ponsardin.[31]

This war of words which went on intermittently for over a hundred years between Champenois and Burgundians bore some of the bitterness characteristic of family feuds. This was not surprising since most of the wines of the two provinces were Pinot wines, by no means identical, of course, although they did share a certain measure of family likeness, whether they were *Pineau de Bourgogne*, *Franc Pineau* or any of the other Pineaux named by Olivier de Serres.[6]

The Champenois appear to have been keener, or at any rate more enterprising than the Burgundians, in their attempts to create a greater demand for their wines in Paris, Flanders and elsewhere, in the few markets within their reach. They spared no trouble or expense to improve the quality of their wines, taking the greatest possible care to choose and press none but the soundest and ripest grapes at the time of the vintage, as well as to introduce better methods of vinification, so that their wines might "travel" better to distant parts and keep longer than they did before. "On commence à vendanger une demi-heure après le lever du soleil, et si le soleil est sans nuages et qu'il soit un peu ardent, sur les neuf ou dix heures, on cesse de vendanger et on fait son sac ou Cuvée: parce que passé cette heure, le raisin étant échauffé, le vin serait coloré ou teint de rouge et demeurerait trop foncé." [41]

But that was not all: the Champenois were also very anxious to have wines to offer to men of fashion, courtiers and the more wealthy wine-lovers, wines that would cost more but also be worth more on account of their novelty. Voltaire evidently heard of this but he apparently failed to grasp what the Champenois were aiming at: he wrote that they had not only planted more vineyards when Louis XIV was king but had taken far greater pains to improve their wines and to produce new ones that had not been known before, giving them the colour, the breed and the body of the wines of Burgundy, so as to sell them profitably abroad. "On a planté plus de vignes et on les a mieux travaillées: on a fait de nouveaux vins qu'on ne connaissait pas auparavant, tels que ceux de Champagne auxquels on a su donner la couleur, la sève, et la force de ceux de Bourgogne et qu'on débite chez l'étranger avec un grand avantage." [39]

The ambition of the Champenois was certainly not to imitate the wines of Burgundy but, on the contrary, to produce wines that "had not been known before". This is why there are so many references, from the second quarter of the seventeenth century onwards, to Champagne of different colours such as *œil de perdrix*, *cerise*, *couleur de miel*, *gris* and *blanc*, that is, partridge-eye or tawny, cherry-pink, honey-blonde, grey and white. This innovation was first recorded by Charles Estienne and his son-in-law Jean Liébault in the 1658 edition of their *L'Agriculture et Maison Rustique* (p. 588.): "Quant à la couleur, aucun est blanc, autre flave ou fauve, ou entre blanc et roux, comme couleur de miel."

It is also referred to in *Manière de cultiver la vigne et de faire le vin en Champagne*, an anonymous MS, the author of which is believed to be the Abbé Godinot:

"Il est vrai qu'il n'y a guère que cinquante ans qu'ils [les Champenois] se sont étudiés à faire du vin gris et presque blanc; mais auparavant leur vin, quoique rouge, était fait avec plus de soin et de propreté que tous les autres vins du royaume." [55]

Also in the *XIIIe Entretien du spectacle de la nature* by Pluche: "Ils [les Champenois] sont parvenus à le rendre [le vin] à volonté couleur de cerise, œil de perdrix, de la dernière blancheur ou parfaitement rouge, et de l'affermir au point que, sans rien perdre de son agrément, il se soutient souvent beaucoup plus." [55]

The *vin gris* or near-white wine which was such a novelty in 1660 in Champagne was a still wine and it was only twenty years later that Dom Pérignon "put the bubbles in", as the making of the first sparkling Champagne at the Abbey of Hautvillers has been sometimes described. Yet, strange as it may seem at first, this *vin gris* of Champagne was first bottled, sold and drunk as a sparkling wine in London during the sixties and seventies of the seventeenth century. The reason for this is obvious: they had corks in London and they had none then in the landlocked province of Champagne.

Wine with some carbon dioxide still in it can be drunk, and used to be drunk straight from the cask during its final stages of fermentation, when from four to six months old. It is quite normal for the fermentation of new wines to be checked by the lower temperature of the winter months, immediately or soon after the vintage, and to start again when spring returns. Francis Scacchus, a Roman doctor, condemned as likely to be injurious to health the practice which had become fashionable in his day of drinking new wine that was lively and semi-sparkling. "An vinum titillans, vulgo piccans, nuncupatium sanitatisit utile." [8]

Wine was first bottled in glass bottles, which were stoppered with cork stoppers, during the reign of Queen Elizabeth I in England, and as there was no such thing as a corkscrew at the time, the smaller end of the cork was driven into the neck of the bottle while an inch or more of the other end stuck out, ready to be pulled out whenever the wine happened to be required. There is, however, no mention of Champagne nor any reference to any sparkling wine, but there was ale bottled in glass bottles, and stoppered with corks "fast tied in with strong Packthread",[2] as early as the reign of Queen Mary, if we are to credit Fuller's story of Dr Alexander Nowell, the Dean of St Paul's, "a dear lover and constant practiser of angling" (according to Izaak Walton) who found "a gun instead of a bottle" on the river bank where he had left, a few days before, a bottle of ale lying on the grass: the cork flew out with a loud bang, much to the Dean's surpise, but he found the ale none the worse.

There is a more detailed account of the sparkling quality of bottled ale in Heywood's *Philocothonista or the Drunkard opened, dissected and anatomized*, published in London in 1635, when the author pretends that he was shot down by bottled ale "with their corks which pealed against me like so many pot-guns".

The earliest records of any bottled wine being sparkling date from the Restoration, although there are numerous references to wine in glass bottles with cork stoppers from the reign of Queen Elizabeth I onwards. There is no better authority than Shakespeare in this as in so many other matters: "Take the cork out of thy mouth that I may drink thy tidings", says Rosalind to Celia, whose stammering comes "as wine out of a narrow mouthed bottle". (*As You Like It, Act III. sc. 2. l.* 213).

It is even likely that there were bad corks and corky wine in 1599 when Jonson's *Cynthia's Revels* was first acted, since we read at the end of the *Introduction*: "a fifth only shakes his bottle-head and out of his corky brain squeezeth not a pitiful learned fact".

There were certainly corks in plenty and in common use in England during the seventeenth century, and, from the middle of the century and at the time of the Restoration, there were also particularly strong, heavy, black glass bottles, so good and so cheap – they cost but two pence – that there was a demand for them on the Continent. This was due, strangely enough, to the concern of Admiral Sir Robert Mansell for the future of the King's Navy. He had been greatly alarmed at the rapid rate of destruction of many forests by the glassmakers, and he feared that before long there would not be any timber for shipbuilding. So he obtained from James I, in 1615, the total prohibition of the use of wood in glass-works furnaces: seacoal had to be used instead, and it proved to be a great deal better than wood. It was then that glass bottles began to be made on a commercial scale in England. Sir Kenelm Digby was granted a patent in 1632, to make a glass wine bottle of his "invention", or design

– the short-necked, bulbous bottle, the easiest for the blower to make, of which many specimens still exist in museums and private collections. Two men who claimed to have worked for Sir Kenelm Digby – Henry Holden and John Colenet – were granted a patent on September 6, 1662, for the sole use of their new "invention for making glass bottles . . ."

So there were in London, at the time of the Restoration, good glass bottles and an abundance of corks, to say nothing of the "packthread" to keep the corks in place, when the Marquis de Sillery sent to his friend St-Evremond the first cask of Champagne to be bottled in England.

Of course, Champagne as a still wine, a red beverage wine, had been heard of in England at least fifty years earlier, in the reign of James I, when Dr Tobias Venner (1575–1660) wrote: "There are also in France wines (would to God they were as common as Claret) which for pleasantnesse of taste, mediocrity of colour, substance and strength, doe for most bodies, for ordinarie use with meate, far excell all other wines: such are chiefly Vin de Coussy et d'Hai, which to the kings and Peeres of France are in very familiar use. They notably comfort the stomacke, help the concoction and distribution of the meates, and offend not the head with vaporous fumes. They are Regall Wines indeede, and very convenient for every season, age and constitution, so they might be had." [7]

Sparkling Champagne, however, had never been heard of or even thought of until the Restoration when it was introduced to the Court and the polite society of London by a remarkable Frenchman called St-Evremond. He had distinguished himself by his bravery as a soldier, by his learning as a philosopher, and by his wit as a courtier when he was chosen to accompany the Comte de Soissons, who was sent to London in 1660 to congratulate Charles II, in the name of Louis XIV, upon his Restoration. The following year, however, St-Evremond incurred the displeasure of Louis and he would probably have spent the rest of his life in the Bastille had he not crossed the Channel in time and come to England, never to return to France. Settling in London, he soon became the arbiter of good taste among the men and women of fashion of the day: the Duke of Buckingham, the Duke of Ormond, the Earl of St Albans, the Earl of Arlington, Lord d'Aubigny, Lord Crofts, and many other such people of high rank were among his friends. With the King himself, St-Evremond was so great a favourite that he was appointed by Royal Commission "Governor of the Duck Islands" with a salary of £300 a year. This "Government" consisted of two or three small islands in St James's Park canal which were used as a decoy for wild duck. And the charm of St-Evremond's personality must have been exceptional since dour Dutch William, William III, always named the old favourite of Charles II as one of the guests whom he would be pleased to meet whenever he dined at a private house.

Fortunately for the people of Champagne, St-Evremond, a Normandy man, loved Champagne above all wines. Before coming to England he had been one of the three original members of the *Ordre des Coteaux*, a group of gourmets of refined and somewhat extravagant tastes, who insisted on having the very best, cost what it might, and as they would not drink, according to the gossips of the day, any other wines than those of Ay, Avenay and Hautvillers, they had been dubbed "Les Coteaux". The Marquis de Sillery, who had vineyards at Avenay and Verzenay, as well as at Sillery, was also a member of *l'Ordre des Coteaux*, and so was the Comte d'Olonne; they were both intimate

Plate 3   VERZENAY. Some of the Verzenay vineyards in the heart of the Montagne de Reims and the Moulin de Verzenay, a very famous Champagne landmark. View taken from Messrs Lanson's Verzenay Vendangeoir.

friends of St-Evremond before he came to England, and it was to them that he wrote from London for supplies of Champagne for himself and for his noble friends. It was quite usual at the time for noble lords and others to import wine direct from the grower: they would also sell some of it to their friends, if it suited them, without any regard whatsoever for the rights and feelings of wine merchants. Thus, for instance, the account in the Fifth Earl of Bedford's Papers, in the Muniments Room at Welbeck Abbey:

> 23 March 1667/68. Paid to Mr Batterleir for the remainder
> of the money due for the Sillery wine
> bought by the Lord Crofts   £12. 10. 0.
> For bottles, corks, drinking glasses,
> bottle brushes, etc.   £18. 11. 4.

The quantities of Champagne which St-Evremond managed to get from his friends in France were never large and they only too frequently failed to arrive, but other courtiers, as well as some of the City merchants, must also have occasionally received supplies of Champagne so that the demand grew very quickly. The wine became rapidly fashionable as a new wine, invariably referred to as being lively and sparkling. In all the accounts which we have been able to find up till now, the cost of the wine, of the bottles and of the corks is given separately, as Champagne was evidently always bought to be immediately bottled and corked:

> 25 March 1665   34s.8d. for Champaign wine, also 2 dozen
>   glass bottles and corks.
> 25 March 1666   Eight gross corks. Six dozen and 3 glass
>   bottles. Twelve dozen stone bottles.
> 25 March 1667   Twelve gross and a half corks. 24 dozen
>   and 3 glass bottles. 30 dozen and 5 stone
>   bottles.
>   A cork tub to keep bottles of [Cham-
>   pagne] wine cool 19s.

(From the Duke of Bedford's Household Accounts at Woburn Abbey.) The earliest printed reference to sparkling Champagne in England that we

know of is in Butler's *Hudibras*, 1664 edition, which bears Roger Lestrange's
imprimatur dated 5 November 1663:

> Drink every letter o'it in stum,
> And make it brisk Champagne become. *Part II. Canto 1. p. 29.*

From that time onwards, mentions of Champagne become more and more
frequent in plays of the time. Thus, Sir George Etheredge, in two of his plays,
She Would if She Could (1668):

> Drink the flask of Champagne,
> Twill serve you for paint and love potion. *Act IV. sc. 2.*

and *The Man of Mode* (1676):

> To the Mall and the park
> Where we love till 'tis dark,
> Then sparkling Champaign
> Puts an end to their reign;
> It quickly recovers poor languishing lovers,
> Makes us frolic and gay, and drowns all sorrow;
> But, alas, we relapse again on the morrow. *Act IV. sc. 1.*

Jack Wildish in *The Mulberry Garden*, first acted on 18 May 1668, sends
Sedley "for a dozen more Champaign".

and in *Doctor and His Patients*:

> One day to call 'em all together
> And one by one he asked 'em whether
> It were not better, by good diet,
> To keep the blood and humours quiet.
> With toast and ale to cool their brain,
> Than nightly fire 'em with Champaign.

Otway, in *Friendship in Fashion*, 1678:

> Under the influence of powerful Champaign, as they call it,
> a spark can no more refrain running into love than a drunken
> country vicar can avoid disputing of religion when his
> patron's ale grows stronger than his reason. *Act III. sc. 1.*

Shadwell, in *The Virtuoso*, 1676:

> . . . come as the sparks do to a playhouse, too full of Champaign,
> venting very much noise and very little wit.   *Act. II. sc. 2.*

Within a dozen years or so of the Restoration, Champagne had not only become the most fashionable wine at Court and among the wealthier members of London Society, but it had also been responsible for a popular demand for sparkling wines of all kinds, wines which were made to order by some of the vintners of the day, according to the author of *The Art and Mystery of Vintners and Wine Coopers, by one who served two apprenticeships to a Vintner in the City of London*, a little book which was printed in London in 1675. "Our wine-coopers of latter times use vast quantities of sugar and molasses to all sorts of wines, to make them drink brisk and sparkling, and to give them spirits, as also to mend their bad tastes, all of which raisins and cute and stum perform."

By the end of the seventeenth century, Champagne was sold in some of the London taverns and coffee-houses, a sparkling wine without any possible doubt, as so amusingly described by Farquhar in his comedy *Love and a Bottle*, *Act II, sc. 2.*, acted in 1697:

B: . . . Champagne is a fine liquor, which all great Beaux drink to make them witty.

M: Oh! By the Universe! I must be witty. I'll drink nothing else. I never was witty in all my life. I love jokes dearly. Here, Club, bring us a bottle of what d'ye call it, the witty liquor.

(*Club, his servant, brings a bottle of Champagne*)

M: Come, fill yourself. (*He fills his glass and drinks.*)
But where's the wit now, Club? Have you found it?

C: Egad! Master, I think 'tis a very good jest.

M: What?

C: What! Why, drinking. You'll find, Master, that this same gentleman in straw doublet, this same Will o'th' Wisp, is a wit at the bottom. (*He refills the glasses.*) Here, here, Master, how it puns and quibbles in the glass!

M: By the Universe, now I have it; the wit lies in the jingling: all wit consists most in jingling. Hear how the glasses rhyme to one another . . . I fancy this same wine is all sold at Will's Coffee-house.

Farquhar's mention of the "straw doublet" might very well mean that, by the closing years of the seventeenth century, the Champagne by then made at Hautvillers by Dom Pérignon was already exported to England, either to Will's Coffee-house or for them. If so, there is no doubt that Will's Coffee-house had the best Champagne in London, a wine made from the cleverly blended wines from various Champagne vineyards by a master.

Incidental evidence of the popularity that Champagne had gained in England during the latter part of the seventeenth century is to be found in a book published by a "Phylo Chemist", George Hartman, "who liv'd and travell'd with the Honourable and Renown'd Sir Kenelm Digby in several parts of Europe, the Space of Seven Years till he died." Hartman's book has its title *The Family Physitian*, and there is in it a chapter entitled "The true English Wine Cellar", in which the author tells the reader how *To make artificial Champagne* "comparable with the best of that which is made in that province".[14]

In England, the sale of Champagne and of all French wines had become increasingly difficult since the reign of James II, when the duty upon all wines from France was raised from £7 per tun to £14, in 1685. According to the incomplete Customs returns of the period, the imports of French wine in England averaged 13,000 tuns per annum from 1690 to 1696, but they declined sharply during the reign of William III, who raised the duty on French wines to £22 in 1693, £47 in 1697 and £51 in 1698. And yet, if tradition is to be trusted, red, still Champagne was the wine which William III preferred. There was no relief when Queen Anne came to the throne: on the contrary, when the Methuen Treaty was signed, in 1703, the duty on French wines was raised to £55 per tun, whereas that on the wines of Portugal remained at the old rate of £7 per tun. But, in spite of this crippling penal taxation, Champagne continued to be available in London and it is often referred to by the rhymsters of the period, mostly as a symbol of extravagance, luxury and affectation:

> From Channel Row he ne'er crost the main,
> Nor from flat Rhenish else reached brisk Champaign.
> *State Poems. London. 1703. Vol. III, p. 385.*

So wrote a jealous very minor poet of Mat Prior, the son of a carpenter, who had risen in the social world as the protégé of the Earl of Dorset.

CHAPTER FOUR

Dom Pérignon and the Eighteenth Century

DOM PÉRIGNON WAS BORN AT Ste-Menehoulde in 1639; he renounced the world at the early age of nineteen, and he died in 1715, having served God to the best of his ability for fifty-five years in the Benedictine Abbey of Hautvillers, high up on the vine-clad slopes rising from the right bank of the Marne, overlooking Epernay upon the other side.

In pre-Revolution France, as in pre-Reformation England, it was left to the religious orders to look after the poor and the sick, which is why so many wealthy people gave them during their lifetime, or bequeathed to them at death, either money or real estate. To this day, in order to carry on their charitable work, the Hospices de Beaune depend upon the income they get each year when they sell by public auction, on the third Sunday in November, the wine made some few weeks before from grapes grown in the vineyards given to them at different times in the course of the last five centuries. Likewise, the Abbey of Hautvillers owned a number of vineyards in the Champagne country, in 1668, when Dom Pérignon was appointed Cellarer, an office which he occupied for forty-seven years, to the day of his death. He had a remarkably sensitive palate and a very keen wine memory, which he retained even in old age, after he had lost his sight. He made better wine than had ever been made before at Hautvillers, rightly blending the wines of different Champagne vineyards into *cuvées*, a technique which has never been improved upon and is still the honoured rule in Champagne today.

The world-wide reputation which Dom Pérignon enjoys today is not, however, due to the fact that he made good wine but to the fiction that he "put bubbles" in Champagne. He did nothing of the sort. What he did was to get, for the first time in Champagne, stoppers made of cork bark, so that he was able in the early spring to bottle the wine of the preceding vintage and to cork it down with corks safely tied down; presently he had sparkling Champagne for sale as a novelty and at a higher price than the still wines of the Abbey. It can be taken for granted that both the still and sparkling Champagnes of the Abbey of Hautvillers, when Dom Pérignon was Cellarer, were better and cheaper than other Champagne wines – better because of the long experience and great skill of Dom Pérignon, and cheaper because they were exempt from the sale and transit taxes which lay merchants were obliged to pay. It is not surprising, therefore, if Dom Pérignon wine, as the Abbey of Hautvillers wines were often called, was popular not only in Champagne but also in Paris. Thus, in his commentary of Boileau's *Ordre des Coteaux*, Brossette gives the names of the Champagne vineyards regarded as the best, at the beginning of the eighteenth century, as follows: Sillery, Verzenay, Ay, Hautvillers, Pérignon, and Saint-Thierry. The good monk had gone to heaven by then but he had become a *coteau*, or vineyard, for the gossip writers of Paris!

By an irony of fate, the sparkling wine which was first made in Champagne, and better made than anywhere else, by a humble and holy country monk, became the fashion – not to say the craze – at the Court of the dissolute, pagan Duc d'Orléans, Regent of France from 1715 to 1723, and then at the Court of his nephew, Louis XV. In her *Letters*, which were published in Hamburg and Paris in 1788, Princess Charlotte Elizabeth of Bavaria, the Regent's mother, wrote on August 13, 1716: "When my son gets drunk, it is not with strong drinks or spirituous liquors but pure wine of Champagne". And, according to St-Simon's *Mémoires*, the Regent rarely went to bed sober. One of his boon companions, the Duc de Richelieu, also records in his *Chroniques* that two bottles of Champagne were enough to unbalance the Regent.

A number of people who had Champagne to sell pretended to have made their wine according to Dom Pérignon's own "secrets", which they had obtained by means fair or foul. One of them was a M. Bidet, "officier du roy" and proprietor of vines at Ay, who gave Dom Pérignon's phoney recipe as follows: "Dans environ une chopine de vin, il faut faire dissoudre une livre de sucre candi, y jeter cinq ou six pêches, séparées de leur noyau, pour environ 4 sols de canelle pulvérisée, une noix muscade aussi en poudre: après que le tout est bien mêlé et dissous, on ajoute un demi-septier de bonne eau-de-vie brûlée, on passe la colature à travers un linge fin et bien net, on jette la liqueur, non le marc, dans la pièce de vin, ce qui le rend délicat et friand." This M. Bidet d'Ay was a different person from his contemporary, M. Bidet de Reims, who wrote a history of Reims.[53]

But there were never any such "secrets" if we are to believe the trustworthy evidence of Dom Grossard, the last *procureur* of the Abbey of Hautvillers, which was secularised at the time of the French Revolution. Dom Grossard wrote to M. d'Herbès, of Ay, from Moutier-en-Der, on October 25, 1821:

"You know, Sir, that it was the famous Dom Pérignon who discovered the secret how to make sparkling white wine, and how to get it clear without having to decant the bottles, as it is done by our big merchants, more often twice than only once, as before him our monks only knew how to make straw or grey wines; and it is also to Dom Pérignon that we owe the cork as now used. To bottle wine, instead of a cork made of cork bark, one only used hemp and after it was dipped in oil it served as a stopper. It was to the "marriage" [blending] of our wines that they owed their goodness. When the vintage was near, Dom Pérignon would say to one of the brothers: 'Go and bring me grapes from Prières, Côtes-à-Bras, Barillets, Quartiers du Clos Ste-Hélène, etc.' Without being told which were the grapes before him, he would tell the brother: 'These are grapes from such or such a vineyard and they must be "married" to those of such and such another vineyard.' And he made no mistake. I do assure you, Sir, that never did we add sugar in our wines, and you can say so to all whenever you happen to be in company when the subject arises." [33]

Sparkling Champagne was *de rigueur* at the Palais Royal parties which, according to public rumour, were mere drinking bouts, or worse. There was probably as much Champagne drunk at Sceaux, where the Duchesse du Maine's Court rivalled that of the Regent, but better manners prevailed.

We may be quite certain that during the course of his long, celibate life, Benedictine Dom Pérignon never for a moment imagined, as he tried so hard to make wine that would be sparkling but not burst its bottles, that it would be so soon acclaimed and abused by women of high rank and low morals.

It was, according to d'Argenson's *Mémoires*, Madame de Mailly, when *maîtresse en titre* of the king, in 1740, who made Louis XV share her love of sparkling Champagne at the *soupers* of the Château de la Muette – just as, incidentally, the Duchesse de Mazarin, one of Charles II's beautiful mistresses, had made him share her and St-Evremond's love of Champagne at her *petits soupers* in the London of the Restoration.

Another fair sinner, Mademoiselle de Navarre, when she was the mistress of Maréchal Maurice de Saxe, had some of her father's sparkling Champagne sent to Brussels, where the Maréchal had his headquarters, in 1745. In 1746, when back at Avenay, she invited the poet Marmontel to come and stay "some months" there, assuring him that there could not be anything better by way of poetical inspiration than her own company and her father's Champagne. The poet came, but not the inspiration – Marmontel's verse is very dull – although there was no lack of Champagne if we are to believe him when he writes that "in the midst of fifty thousand bottles of Champagne, it was difficult not to lose one's head". [34]

Dom Pérignon died in 1715, and by that time the demand for sparkling Champagne had become sufficiently important to tempt a number of vineyard proprietors to bottle some of their wine in the early spring, that it might finish fermenting after being corked down and so become sparkling. Such were the Vicomte de Puisieulx, the eldest son of the Marquis de Sillery, Monsieur de Navarre at Avenay, the Vicomte de Brimont at Reims, Claude Moët and Bertin du Rocheret at Epernay, as well as, very likely, a number of others whose names have not come down to us.

According to Chaptal [21], the quantities of Champagne exported during the years 1720 to 1725 averaged 2,710 casks and 30,220 bottles to foreign parts, and 6,600 bottles to the French colonies.

As evidence of the importance of the trade in sparkling Champagne some

ten years after Dom Pérignon's death, we have the request of the Mayor and
Echevins of Reims to the King, asking that the Champenois be allowed to send
their bottled wines in osier baskets or hampers to Normandy and to the ports
of Rouen, Caen, Dieppe and le Havre for shipment abroad: they stated that
the trade in the wines of Champagne had increased considerably during the
past few years, as a result of the greater care and skill of the *vignerons*, who now
bottled wines during the time of the first March moon after the vintage, so
that they would become sparkling: and all the people who drink Champagne
gris (off-white) prefer it to be sparkling rather than not; besides which, no *vin
gris* can be sent to any part of France, and still less to foreign countries, without
losing completely its quality if sent in casks. This request of the Reims muni-
cipality was duly granted by a decree of May 25, 1728, "de faire arriver en
bouteilles, dans la Province de Normandie, pour la consommation des habitants
d'icelle, du vin de Champagne gris en paniers, qui ne pourront être moindres
de cent bouteilles . . . ou pour être embarqués pour l'étranger dans les ports
de Rouen, Caen, Dieppe et le Havre, et non dans aucuns autres ports".[11]

Of all the *vignerons* and merchants who made and sold Champagne during
the eighteenth century, there are two who have left us a great deal of first-
hand information – they are Bertin du Rocheret and Claude Moët, both of
Epernay.

Bertin du Rocheret was born at Epernay in 1693, the son of Adam Bertin,
Sieur du Rocheret, Président de l'Election d'Epernay – the first citizen of
Epernay, who owned vineyards, chiefly at Ay. The son, Philippe-Valentin, was
educated by the Jesuits at their Reims College: he then went to Paris, studied
law, was called to the Paris Bar but returned to Epernay in 1717, the year of
his father's death, and was elected Président et Grand Voyeur de l'Election
d'Epernay in place of his father. A man of exceptional energy, he also had the
rare gift of making and keeping friends. The Maréchal de Montesquiou d'Artagnan, who commanded the Mousquetaires du Roi, was one of his best
friends – and customers. It was through him that Bertin came to know a number of young Mousquetaires and among them the sons of some Jacobite exiles,
such as Sir Richard Bulstrode and Colonel Parker, better known in Paris
as Milord Parker. Somehow or other, this "Milord" Parker got involved in
some unpleasant lawsuit and Bertin was able to get him out of it – a service

which Parker's two sons, one an admiral and the other a general, and his kinsman Thomas Parker, Lord Chief Justice of England, repaid by buying Bertin's Champagne and getting their friends in England to do the same.

Another good friend whom Bertin made during his Paris days was the Chevalier de Besvres, better known as Monsieur de Chavigny, Envoy Extraordinary to the Court of St James until the death of George I, in 1727, and again from 1732 to 1736, when George II was king.

In spite of his official duties and a voluminous correspondence with his many friends and acquaintances, among whom were famous people such as Voltaire, Crébillon, Adrienne Le Couvreur, Stanislas, the Duc de Lorraine (ex-King of Poland), the Abbé Bignon, Bibliothécaire du Roi, and many others, Bertin du Rocheret managed to attend to what must have been the most flourishing business in Champagne at the time.

Both Bertin du Rocherets, father and son, sold some sparkling Champagne, because their customers demanded it, but they did not like it at all. In a letter which he wrote on October 18, 1713, to the Maréchal de Montesquiou d'Artagnan, Bertin du Rocheret *père* says that the only merit of the early bottled wine, which he is sending him, is to be sparkling, a merit which, in his (Bertin's) opinion, is that of wines of little worth, and belongs to beer, chocolate and whipped cream. He ends by saying that sparkling wine has a taste of "working" or fermenting and that if it be sparkling at all, it is because it is still working or fermenting. "Ils ont été mis en bouteilles en même temps que celui que vous avez, afin que votre vin fût mousseux, sans quoi je ne l'aurais pas fait mettre, et vous auriez pu le trouver meilleur; mais il n'aurait pas eu le mérite du mous-sage qui, selon moi, est un mérite de petit vin, et le propre de la bière, du chocolat et de la crême fouettée. Le bon vin de Champagne doit être clair, fin, pétiller dans le verre, et flatter ce qu'on appelle le bon goût, qu'il n'a jamais quand il mousse, mais bien un goût de travail et de vandage; aussi ne mousse-t-il qu'à cause qu'il travaille." [53]

On October 25, 1713, the Maréchal replied to Bertin and begins his letter with: "I see now how wrong I was to ask you to bottle my wine so that it would be sparkling; it is a fashion which rules everywhere, but more particu-larly among the younger generation; but I am delighted to know what you have written to me about the *mousse*, and I promise you that in future I shall not mention it again". [49]

In 1716, Bertin du Rocheret sold to his friend the Maréchal de Montesquiou d'Artagnan 1,500 bottles of Champagne at 35 sols per bottle in bin Epernay. In 1725, he quoted his *flacons blancs mousseux liqueur* at 50 sols and *ambrés non mousseux* at 25 and 30 sols per *flacon*. In 1734, he sent to the Marquis de Polignac some *mousseux* and some *pétillant* Champagne, and, in 1735, he refers to his Ay *mousseux* and to his *saute-bouchon* at from 45 to 50 sols per *flacon*. The next year, however, owing probably to a particularly high percentage of burst bottles, his *saute-bouchon* had gone up to 3 livres and 6 sols, the *mousseux* to 42 sols, the *bon mousseux* from 45 to 50 sols, and the *demi-mousseux* from 36 to 40 sols. The next year, in 1737, the *saute-bouchon* cost 3 livres and 6 sols, and the *mousseux* 42 sols.

In a letter dated December 20, 1736, the Abbé Bignon acknowledges receipt of some Champagne which Bertin du Rocheret had sent him, some with red wax being *sablant* but not *mousseux*, some with black wax "furiously green" and with little vinosity; but three spoonfuls at the bottom of a glass filled the glass to the brim with *mousse*. In another letter, the same Abbé Bignon refers to the "fizzy verjuice" for which some people are willing to pay more than for really good Champagne wine.

On January 22, 1734, Abbé Bignon wrote to Bertin fils; "The less *mousseux* and appealing to the eyes of our coquettes the wine will be, and the more it will have at first what you are pleased to call liqueur and I prefer to call balsamic parts, the more shall I appreciate it. Moins le vin sera mousseux et étincelant aux yeux de nos coquettes de table, et plus au contraire il aura dans ces commencements cy de ce qu'il vous plaît d'appeler liqueur, et qu'en termes chimistes j'appellerai plustot des parties balsamiques, plus j'en ferai de cas." [52]

In 1738, Bertin despatched 30 casks of Champagne from Epernay to Monsieur de Castagnet in Paris, *pour les petits soupers du roi*, some of the wine to be drunk *en nouveau* and the rest to be bottled.

Bertin certainly had quite a number of customers in England where he appointed an agent, Chabane, the first Champagne agent on record, to whom he wrote on October 16, 1725, giving him the prices of the 1725 vintage as follows: *Les flacons blancs mousseux trente, quarante et cinquante sols, les ambrés non mousseux, sablant, vingt-cinq sols*. (Bottles of white, sparkling, liqueured wine, 30, 40 and 50 sols per bottle. Amber, non-sparkling, beeding, 25 sols.)

Bertin also gave Chabane detailed directions as to when and how he was to bottle the wine which was sent to him in casks. Thus, in a letter from Epernay dated November 29, 1729, Bertin informs Chabane that he is going to send him some wine from the Clos St-Pierre, *pour boire en nouveau*. In another of his letters to Chabane from Epernay, dated September 9, 1731, he recommends the use of some cream of tartar to ensure a greater limpidity of the wine at the time of bottling. A few weeks later, on October 13, he writes again to Chabane and tells him that he is sending him some cream of tartar, in case none was available in London.

After the Peace of Aix-la-Chapelle, in 1748, which brought to an end the war of the Austrian Succession, the shipping of Champagne to England must have become a much more important affair, to judge from a letter which Bertin wrote to the Marquis de Clavières, in 1749, in which he says that *"les Champenois font payer la guerre aux Anglais"*.

Next to George II, the Earl of Chesterfield was Bertin's best customer in England: this nobleman, who was Steward of the Household of George II,

was a magnificent host, the arbiter of fashion and a great lover of Champagne.
It was the wine he always chose to toast the most beautiful women of the day,
always with much wit, and sometimes with cruel sarcasm.

> "Give me Champagne and fill it to the brim,
> I'll toast in bumpers ev'ry lovely limb,
> I challenge all the heroes of the skies
> To show a goddess with a Craven's eyes."
>
> *Lord Chesterfield's Witticisms or the Grand*
> *Pantheon of Genius, Sentiments and Taste.*
> *London. 1773 edition. p. 130.*

On October 12, 1754, Bertin wrote for the last time to Chabane telling him
that the wines of 1753 were remarkable and that they "embaument aussi bien
qu'en 1743": he also told him that his best Cuvée of Ay 1753 had been reserved entirely for George II and Stanislas, the king of Poland in exile. Bertin
retired in 1754, and he died at Epernay in 1762.

Bertin never had a good word for the wine he called *saute-bouchon*, the sort
of Champagne that had no better recommendation than its gas. He sold Ay
wine that was *crémant* or *sablant*, lively but not *frénétique*, as he called the "frenzied" *saute-bouchon*. Much to his sorrow, the fashion, not to say the craze, for
sparkling Champagne in Paris had sent prices rocketting and there were people
foolish enough to pay such prices for new and acid young white wines with
no merit except that they were full of gas. Writing in 1744, Bertin records in
his *Journal* that Avize was at the time quite an important *bourg* and that it had
grown considerably during the previous twelve or fifteen years, owing to the
"frenzied invention of sparkling wine". Before 1710, adds Bertin, Avize was
a poor village and nearly all its vineyards were planted with white grape vines;
they produced only a little wine, which was acid and had a rasping taste. It
was considered one of the least of Champagne wines – so much so, that it sold
at from 25 to 30 livres per *queue* (two hogsheads); but since the craze of the
saute-bouchon, that "abominable drink", the same wine fetched up to 300 livres,
and vineyards which found no buyers at 250 livres per *arpent*, now sold for
as much as 2,000 livres; as a result Avize, with its many handsome new houses,
acquired an entirely new look.

Avize est un bourg assez considérable, extrêment augmenté depuis douze ou quinze ans environ par la frénétique invention du vin mousseux. Il était encore pauvre en 1710 ... Leurs vignes, presque toutes plantées en ceps blancs, ne leur produisaient qu'un petit vin aigre et d'un goût raîche qui le faisait réputer un des moindres du pays, aussi ne se vendait-il ordinairement que 25 ou 30 livres la queue, mais depuis la manie du saute-bouchon, cette abominable boisson encore plus rebutante par un acide insupportable, se vend jusqu'à 300 livres et l'arpent de vigne dont on ne voulait pas à 250 livres, a été porté jusqu'à 2,000 livres; aussi Avize est-il orné depuis quelque temps d'une quantité de belles maisons de vendange qui en ont absolument changé la face. [54]

In spite of Bertin du Rocheret, *père et fils*, in spite of the Abbé Bignon and others who did not like the *mousse*, and said so, sparkling Champagne became more and more popular in France and elsewhere. Voltaire, Madame de Pompadour, Madame du Chatelet, the Duc de Richelieu loved it; so did Frederick I of Prussia and the first three Georges of England.

> Chloris, Eglé me versent de leur main
> D'un vin d'Ay dont la mousse pressée,
> De la bouteille avec force élancée,
> Comme un éclair fait voler son bouchon.
> Il part, on rit; il frappe la plafond:
> De ce vin frais l'écume pétillante
> De nos Français est l'image brillante.
>> *Voltaire. Le Mondain. 1736*

According to the Châlons-sur-Marne records, the quantities of Champagne entered at the Excise Office of that city for export, in 1747 and 1748, were as follows:

Destination	1747	1748
Allemagne	1,555 poinçons & 73,136 bouteilles	1,766 poinçons & 38,608 bouteilles

Plate 4 VILLERS-MARMERY at the eastern end of the Montagne de Reims. The black specks in the rows of green vines are men and women picking the grapes.

Angleterre	1,700 bouteilles à 40 sols	54 pièces & 6,690 bouteilles
Espagne	1,009 bouteilles à 40 sols	1,608 bouteilles
Italie	7,280 bouteilles	1 pièce & 5,130 bouteilles
Flandre	486 poinçons à 100 livres 484 poinçons à 90 livres 18,059 bouteilles à 40 sols	1,138 pièces 15,387 bouteilles
Hollande	49 poinçons & 40,791 bouteilles	28 pièces & 8,628 bouteilles
Portugal	1 poinçon & 1,934 bouteilles	1,540 bouteilles

Bottles at 40, 35 and 30 sols.
Poinçons at 145, 140, 110, 100, 90 and 75 livres.

Thirty years later, in 1778, the figures relating to the total exports of Champagne are given by Chaptal as follows: [21]

Allemagne	156 poinçons; 5,361 pièces & 165,944 bouteilles
Angleterre	283 muids
Danemark	66 muids
Flandre	843 poinçons; 657 pièces & 23,894 bouteilles
Hollande	6,788 bouteilles
Nord	120 muids
Russie	151 muids
Suède	4 muids
Iles	698 bouteilles
Italie	1,858 bouteilles
Suisse	5,298 bouteilles

In 1788, the export totals were 387,247 *muids* and 319,000 *bouteilles* to foreign lands, and 171,880 *muids* to the Colonies.

Although we do not know who was the shipper of the wine, we can be quite sure that there was Champagne in 1790 in New York, then the national capital. The evidence for this is a letter, published by Stephen Decatur in *Private affair of George Washington* (p. 123), which was written on March 4th 1790 by Senator Johnson, one of the Senators from South Caroline, who had dined on that day with George Washington: "I have just left the President's where I had the pleasure of dining with almost every member of the Senate. We had some excellent Champagne and after it I had the honour of drinking coffee with his lady, a most amiable woman." There is also in the same book (p. 255) an entry referring to the payment of 66 shillings for the "drayage" or transport of "six hampers of champagne wine from the vessel".

In January 1794, when war once more broke out between France and England, the shipping of Champagne became very hazardous and M. Moët appointed an agent in London, a Mr John Motteux, to whom he shipped wine from le Havre to Southampton via Guernsey. In June 1799, Motteux wrote to Epernay complaining of the delay in the delivery of his last order and asking for a further supply of Sillery Champagne "provided its safe arrival can be guaranteed". He added, "There is nothing to be compared to Sillery when it is genuine: it must not have the least sweetness or mousse."

Unlike M. Moët, the Marquis de Sillery – or rather his executor or "steward", M. Mittoux – refused to ship any more Champagne to England and he appointed as his agent in London a Mr Dupuis, with instructions to sell at best by auction what was left of the stocks of Sillery Champagne which the late Marquis had shipped to London before the declaration of war. Hence the advertisement published in *The Times* on February 12, 1794:

"The public are informed that a few cases of this justly celebrated wine may still be had at Mr Dupuis, No 51 Jermyn Street, the corner of Duke Street, St James's, where for the future it will be sold and nowhere else in England or France, the proprietors being bound by this agreement under a penalty of £500. The wine being packed up at Sillery in cases of 60 bottles each under the immediate inspection of Mr Mittoux, agent to the late M. de Sillery, and by him forwarded to London, enables Mr Dupuis not only to sell it cheaper,

but also to warrant it being of the first growth and of that year's vintage marked on each case, and engages to take back the wine should it prove otherwise."

The Vicomte de Puisieulx, in the lifetime of his father, the Marquis de Sillery, also sold Champagne to friends in England, and to others through his friends, such as the Earl of March, who wrote to George Selwyn in November 1766: "I have not yet received some Champagne that Monsieur de Puisieulx has sent me."

All through the eighteenth century, much of the Champagne consumed in England was still being shipped direct by noble vineyard-owners as it had been in the beginning, when St-Evremond introduced the wine of the then Marquis de Sillery to his friends at the Court of Charles II. Here is the translation of a letter written from Epernay on March 1, 1771, to a Mr Phelps in London, which is of interest as showing how much trading methods and conditions differed from those of today:

"Sir and dear friend,

I have just despatched the 500 bottles of Champagne wine, as desired by you, in four hampers, each containing 125 bottles, and I have addressed them to Mr Morel, Commercial Counsellor and merchant at Dunkirk. They are marked M.C.G.4. I have also sent him a small barrel containing four dozen and a half Bon Chre[s]tien winter pears and a small box of dried Rousselet pears, marked in the same way as the hampers, which my wife wishes you to accept with her compliments. I instructed him to forward them as soon as they reach him by the first boat to Mr Charles Green, London Customs House, as you told me. I have paid all charges and shall pay all that the Dunkirk broker may demand, so that you will only have to pay in francs the cost of the wine.

This wine is, I have no hesitation to state, the finest available, and M. de Puisieulx has not tasted any better for the last six years. It is all that I had left. One would give 20 francs a bottle for a hamper of the same wine, or of a wine approaching it in excellence, and I am not afraid to say that one could not find it. All the bottles bear my seal so that they cannot be tampered with.

I beg of you, therefore, to show it to as many of your friends as you can. First of all, of course, to Lord Hitchingbrooke, who has asked for it. I am sure that Lord Sandwich, his father, will also appreciate it – to Lord Halifax, who has asked for it, and, please, let Mr de Rickaby taste it: also I beg of you to assure these noble lords that they shall always have the very best we have.

The price, including all charges, as I have mentioned to you, is five livres ten sols (about 4s.6d.) per bottle, that is for the 500 bottles, 2,750 livres or 114½ Louis.

If I can be of service to your friends to obtain for them any Burgundy, and only the very best, I am quite able to do so, and it will be a great pleasure for me, even if they should require some Muscat. I have good friends in Burgundy upon whom I can thoroughly rely, and I am only 25-30 leagues away.

As soon as your small barrel reaches you, please have the fruit out and in the air. My wife also sends a cask of pears to Lady Egerton and I am sending a hamper of *vin gris* to her husband, both have been sent to Calais as they had not given me any instructions for Dunkirk.

I hope to hear from you soon whether you have settled or not with my firm for your friend's son.

Again let me impress upon you that you are welcome to all I have and that the more you will give me cause to prove to you my friendship, the better you will oblige me . . ."

When the Maréchale d'Estrées died, in 1785, the direct line of the Bruslart de Sillery became extinct: the Château de Sillery and its vineyards passed to another branch, to the Comte Bruslart de Genlis, who carried on the old Sillery tradition of selling Champagne direct to noble lords in England. Thus we read in two of the letters written by George Kendall, in 1786, to the Duke of Rutland, and published in the *Rutland Papers*:

17 August 1786. "I have written also to Comte de Genlis, the present possessor of Sillery, to despatch 500 bottles of his best wines . . ."

20 December 1786. "There are 500 bottles of Sillery Champagne of the very best quality in the proprietor's possession. 300 bottles of Hautvillers Champagne, the growth preferred in Paris to every other; I had it directly from the Prior of that Convent by the Archbishop of Narbonne's intercession; if it is not perfect of its kind, the Prior must be damned for perjury, for he has solemnly declared it to be so . . ."

Sparkling Champagne had been hailed with unbounded enthusiasm when it first "sparkled" in London in the sixties of the seventeenth century and in Paris twenty odd years later, but it was not very long before a reaction set in and still Champagne was for years in much greater demand than sparkling.

In England, Dr Edward Barry shared to the full Bertin du Rocheret's distaste of the *saute-bouchon*: "For some years past, the French and the English have been particularly fond of the sparkling, frothy Champagne. The former have almost entirely quitted that depraved taste, nor does it now so much prevail here. They used to mix some ingredients to give them that quality; but this is unnecessary, as they are too apt spontaneously to run into that state; but whoever chooses to have such wines may be assured that they will acquire it by bottling them at any time after the vintage, before the month of the next May; and the most sure rule to prevent that disposition is to bottle them before the November following. The rule has been confirmed by repeated experiments. The Champaign wines are light and generous, and after they have acquired a firm maturity, are very salutary".[19]

The red wines of Champagne, wines not unlike those of Burgundy, were more popular in England during the eighteenth century than sparkling Champagne, according to the poems, plays, letters and wine-lists of the period. Instead of "sparkling", "lively", "brisk", "foaming", epithets which almost invariably used to be tacked on to Champagne soon after the Restoration, Champagne and Burgundy are nearly always bracketed together. They are, for instance, the first wines offered to guests entering a tavern:

> Name, Sirs, the wine that most invites your taste,
> Champagne or Burgundy, or Florence pure,
> Or Hock antique, or Lisbon new or old,
> Bordeaux, or neat French wine, or Alicant.
> *Wine: a Poem. John Gay. 1708*

Dean Swift pretended not to care for Champagne but it was most likely its price that he objected to, and he mentions Champagne in his letters to Stella, often bracketing it with Burgundy:

> Dined with Mr Secretary St John, and staid till seven, but would not drink his Champaign and Burgundy for fear of the gout.
>
> *Swift's Journal to Stella, March 18, 1710*

Always greatly concerned about his health, Swift wrote to Stella that at dinner he would not drink more than "three or four glasses of Champaign by perfect teasing". (As above, March 29, 1711.)

The following week, having called to see "Mr Secretary St John, who had been very ill with gravel and pains in the back by Burgundy and Champaign, added to the sitting up all night at business, found him drinking tea, whilst the rest were at Champaign." (As above, April 7, 1711.)

The poor Dean was so shocked at the sight of his friend's suffering that the next day, at dinner, he refused to be "teased" into drinking three or four glasses of Champaign without water. (As above, April 9, 1711.)

In one of Vanburgh's comedies, Lady Headpiece reproaches her husband for letting their son drink Port:

> Well, I wonder, Sir Francis, you will encourage that lad to swill such beastly, lubberly liquor. If it were Burgundy or Champagne, something might be said for it; they'd perhaps give him some art and spirit.
>
> *A Journey to London. Act I. sc.2. 1720*

And the perforcedly abstemious Pope, writing from London:

> I sit up till two o'clock over Burgundy and Champagne.
>
> *Letter to Congreve. April 7, 1715*

A little later, Fielding, in one of his plays, has a lady send her servant to the wine-merchant for the wines she wishes to give her guests:

> Go to Mr Mixture, the wine-merchant, and order him to send in twelve dozen of his best Champagne, twelve dozen of Burgundy, and twelve of Hermitage.
>
> *The Miser. 1732*

In the accounts of the first Earl of Bristol (1720-1739) a sum of £30.1.0d. was paid for "Champagne and Burgundy", the two wines being bracketed together.[13]

At the Vauxhall Gardens, in 1762, Champagne and Burgundy top the wine-list at 8s. per bottle (Champagne) and 6s. per bottle (Burgundy), while Claret and "Old Hock" are quoted at 5s., "Rhenish with sugar" at 2s.6d., Mountain (Malaga) at 2s.6d., Red Port and Sherry at 2s. Forty years later, still at Vauxhall Gardens, Burgundy is quoted at 15s., Champagne "Red or White" and "Old Hock" at 14s., Moselle at 12s., Claret, Sauternes and Barsac at 10s., Madeira at 8s., Port, Sherry, Bucellas and Lisbon at 6s.

In spite of its high cost, or maybe because of it, Champagne was at all times the fashionable wine. In London it was mostly sold in places of entertainment like the Pantheon in Oxford Street, where the more dissipated and wealthy men about town flocked on masquerade nights, and where, according to a contemporary eye-witness, "the Champaign made some eyes sparkle that nothing else could brighten". And there were in London, at the time, a number of "Gardens", the smartest of them being the Mulberry, Vauxhall and Spring Gardens, where dancing and drinking were not at the mercy of the weather but carried on indoors. According to *England's Gazeteer* for 1751, "Foxhall was frequented by most of the nobility and gentry then in and near London, being often honoured with some of the Royal Family". In many of his letters, Sir Horace Walpole gives graphic descriptions of suppers at Vauxhall Gardens during the summer months: they evidently did not suffer in those days from licensing restrictions, since suppers usually started at about eleven and lasted till half-past one or sometimes a good deal later, gaiety and gallantry being the rule and Champagne the wine. Of course, the pleasure Gardens of London had but a short season, from May to September, but there were taverns and clubs where drinking and gambling could be enjoyed at all times. Wattier's, White's and Brooks's were the three most fashionable of the West End Clubs. Brooks's was particularly famous for its cellar: it was originally established in Pall Mall, in 1764, by Almack, who also owned the Thatched House. A few years later, however, it was acquired by a wine-merchant, Brooks, who appears to have been also a money-lender. It is hardly likely that he could have become rich enough solely by the sale of wine to build, as he did in 1778, the handsome club house which bears his name at No. 60 St James's Street. Tickell, in an invitation to dinner supposed to have been sent by Fox, wrote:

> Derby shall send, if not his plate, his cooks,
> And know I've bought the best Champagne from Brooks.
> *Tickell's Poems. Epistle from the Hon. Charles Fox*
> *(partridge shooting) to the Hon. John Townsend (cruising).*

Much of the Champagne that reached England during the eighteenth century was drunk in London but it was also in evidence at Bath, where "persons of distinction" flocked for the benefit of their health and also to have a gay time. According to Foote, the satirist, Champagne was part of the Bath Waters cure (*The Fair Maid of Bath. Act. 1. sc. 1. 1771*). Twenty years later, Holcroft makes Harry Dorton console himself by ordering "Champagne and two rummers" (*The Road to Ruin. Act. IV. sc. 2. 1792*). There were other watering places at the time in England which were fashionable, though not so fashionable as the Bath of Beau Nash; at Tunbridge Wells, Buxton and Scarborough, for instance, we have no records of Champagne being on sale.

CHAPTER FIVE

The
Pioneers

BEFORE LEAVING THE EIGHTEENTH CENTURY for what may be called the modern history of Champagne, it is only right that a few words of homage be paid to the pioneers of the Champagne trade, who succeeded in making sparkling Champagne of a quality which appealed to the great and the rich of the day before there were *pupitres* for *remuage*, before the *dégorgement* technique had been thought of, and at a time of ruinous *casse*, when there was no reliable method for ascertaining the sugar content of new wines. And they did more: in days when publicity did not exist, and when means of transport were costly as well as hazardous, they managed somehow to create a demand for Champagne not only in France, but in most Continental capitals, as well as in England, Ireland and the States, before they were United.

The most colourful of those pioneers, and also the most remarkably successful was a young woman, Mademoiselle Ponsardin, who was born at Reims in 1777, and who married, in 1794, Monsieur Clicquot, a Champagne shipper whose firm was founded at Reims in 1772. He must have been quite an enterprising Champagne shipper to judge from the correspondence (still in the firm's archives) with American customers prior to the French Revolution, and from copies of invoices for wine shipped in 1782, 1786, 1788 and 1789. When Monsieur Clicquot died, in 1796, the wise old men of Reims most likely predicted that his firm would soon die. If they did, they were wrong. The young widow – she was not yet twenty – stepped forward and proved herself a most capable business woman in an age when there were few women in business: it was also at one of the most troubled periods of France's history, when the young widow had to face not only civil commotions, war taxation, enemy invasion and occupation, but a chaotic currency, when the old *écus* disappeared and worthless *assignats* were legal tender before francs and centimes became law. Yet, in spite of all manner of difficulties, this remarkable young woman managed her affairs so well that, in 1820, at the early age of 43, she retired *après fortune faite*, to live in great comfort and gracious style for nearly half a century at her Château de Boursault, where she died in 1866. Madame Clicquot had no son and no nephew to carry on the name – she only had one daughter, who married the Comte de Chevigné – and she was in business less than twenty-five years, yet her name has been synonymous with Champagne to this day in every part of the civilized world. She was fortunate, of course, in her father, Monsieur Ponsardin, who was mayor of Reims during the reign of Napoleon: he was probably of great assistance to her. And she was fortunate in her partner, a Monsieur Werler from Wetzlar on the Lahn, in Germany. He, too, was a remarkable person: he became a naturalized Frenchman, gave his name a French accent, Werlé, and was not only chosen by the people of Reims to be their *Maire*, and the President of their Chamber of Commerce, but also their Member of Parliament. At Madame Clicquot's death, in 1866, Monsieur Werlé senior and his son, Comte Alfred Werlé, became sole proprietors of the firm, which by that time had become, under the able management of the Werlés, father and son, the leading Champagne shipper of Reims.

There were other Champagne "widows" in the course of the nineteenth century, the most dynamic of them being Madame Pommery; and there are Champagne widows today as well, Madame Bollinger being the best known of them; but throughout the length and width of the English-speaking world, whoever calls for a bottle of "the Widow" expects to be given a bottle of Champagne that bears the name of the Veuve Clicquot-Ponsardin.

Monsieur Werlé must have been an exceptionally gifted man. But quite a number of other Germans came to Reims, Avize and Ay, primarily as foreign correspondence clerks, "since it is practically impossible for our merchants to find any Frenchmen with a knowledge of foreign languages", according to Max Sutaine, in his *Essai sur l'histoire du vin de Champagne* (p. 105). Quite a few of these Germans never went back to Germany but started in business on their own account and founded the firms of Champagne shippers, which bear to this day the German names of their founders.

Such, for instance, was Florenz Heidsieck, who began trading on his own account at Reims in 1785, and was joined by his nephew, Charles Heidsieck, twenty years later, in 1805. In 1834, at the time of François's discovery and the birth of the Champagne trade as we know it today, the original firm went into voluntary liquidation, and it was so reconstructed that today there are three firms entitled to sell Champagne bearing the names of Heidsieck: Messrs Heidsieck & Co. – Heidsieck Monopole – Messrs Piper-Heidsieck; and Messrs Charles Heidsieck & Co., the last one being the only one owned and managed by members of the Heidsieck family.

There are still older firms of Champagne shippers, both in Reims and Epernay, such as Lanson Père et Fils, of Reims, founded in 1750 by one François Delamotte and a M. Lanson, who changed the style of the firm from Delamotte Père et Fils to Lanson Père et Fils, in 1838, when the last of the Delamottes died.

Older still, in fact the oldest of all the surviving Champagne shippers of the eighteenth century, are Ruinart Père et Fils. They still own a *gros livre de comptes* – whether the firm's first or not they cannot tell – which was started on September 1, 1729. In that year, a cloth merchant of Epernay called Nicolas Ruinart (one of whose uncles, Dom Thierry Ruinart, was a Benedictine monk at Hautvillers at the same time as Dom Pérignon) owned a vineyard and perhaps sold his wine to the clients who bought his cloth, and an old ledger shows that as time went on the sales of cloth decreased as the sales of Champagne increased. Thus in 1764, Nicolas Ruinart's tenth son, Claude, was fully engaged in the making and selling of Champagne, having handed over to other members of the family the cloth business. When his father died, in 1769, Claude transferred the headquarters of his firm, now "Ruinart Pere et Fils", to Reims, where it has been ever since. Claude's eldest son, J.–F. Irénée Ruinart, who succeeded him, was Mayor of Reims in 1811 and *Député de la Marne* from 1815 to 1830.

Second only in seniority, but first in fame and importance today, is the firm known the world over as Moët et Chandon. It was founded in 1743 by Claude Louis Nicolas Moët, a young contemporary of Bertin du Rocheret who owned a number of vineyards near Epernay and devoted the whole of his time and energy to making and selling Champagne, both still and sparkling. In 1743,

he despatched a number of bottles of Champagne of the 1741 vintage to sundry wine-merchants in Paris, and to a Sieur Compoin, Mine Host of the Hôtellerie de la Petite Ecurie at Nantes. A little later, between 1750 and 1762, there are a large number of entries in his ledgers, some of them still in the safe keeping of his successors, showing that he had customers in London, Berlin, Frankfort on Oder, Königsberg and Stettin, Vienna, Brussels, Amsterdam and Russia, as well as in France. On March 11, 1750, for instance, he despatched 2 poin-çons of Champagne to a Mr Gruppty, in London; on August 25, 1755, 360 bottles of Champagne to a Mr Dameroux, of Frankfort on Oder; on February 26, 1760, 120 bottles to the Marquis de Soto Mayor, Madrid; on July 29, 1762, 300 bottles to Dunkirk for Russia; on September 5, 1762, 300 bottles to Calais and 300 bottles to Dunkirk for England; on October 18, 1762, 840 bottles to James Rocols of the St James Coffee House, London.

In 1780, Monsieur Moët bottled 50,000 bottles of sparkling wine, a record at the time. His son, Jean-Rémy, was born in 1758 at Epernay. When he was married, in 1792, his father, Claude, retired and handed him the reins. During the ensuing forty years, Jean-Rémy Moët conducted brilliantly the affairs of his firm; he bought the buildings and vineyards of the famous Hautvillers Abbey, secularised at the time of the French Revolution; he also found time to look after, in a most efficient manner, the affairs of his native Epernay as mayor for many years. Napoleon I, the most distinguished of the many distinguished visitors whom Jean-Rémy Moët entertained during his mayoralty, himself gave the accolade to his host and friend when Jean-Rémy became a Chevalier de la Légion d'Honneur.

In 1832, Jean-Rémy Moët retired and handed over the management of the firm to his son Victor and to his son-in-law, Pierre-Gabriel Chandon, the husband of his only daughter, Adélaïde. He died at Epernay in 1833.

Jean-Rémy Moët, like his father Claude before him, sold both still and spark-ling Champagne to both private clients and wine-merchants. In 1788, for instance, he supplied two hampers, each containing 10 dozen "Vin de Champagne of good quality, not too charged with liqueur, but of excellent taste, and not at all sparkling", to "Milord" Farnham and to Messrs Charbonell, Moody & Walker. In October 1788, the "Chevalier" Colebrook wrote from Bath to Monsieur Moët at Epernay, asking him to send six dozen bottles of Champagne to his friend the Hon. John Butler of Dublin who, he adds, "if satisfied with the wine will become a good customer, being rich and keeping a good house, where he receives many amateurs of Vin de Champagne". To the "Chevalier" himself, M. Moët sent 50 bottles of still Champagne of the 1783 vintage. Another of M. Moët's London customers was a "Milord" Findlater who, in 1789, was sent 10 dozen bottles of sparkling Champagne of the 1788 vintage. In March

1790, a Mr Manning, Mine Host of the St Albans Tavern, was invoiced for 130 bottles of Champagne at 3 Livres (two shillings per bottle), and in April of the same year 30 dozen of Moët's 1788 vintage were invoiced to a Mr Lockart, banker, of 36 Pall Mall, at the equivalent of three shillings per bottle.

On May 17, 1790, a M. Jeanson, who had been sent on several occasions to England by M. Moët, wrote to him from London: "How the taste of this country has altered during the last ten years! Almost everywhere they ask for a dry wine; but they want a wine so vinous and so strong that there is hardly anything but Sillery that will satisfy them."

England at the time was M. Moët's best export market, but there are many entries in his ledgers relating to shipments to both continental Europe and North America. Thus, for instance, 100 bottles *vin mousseux* despatched on September 10, 1787, to a M. Vandalle, wine-merchant at Dunkirk, for shipment to America *à compte à demy*; or 216 bottles, in three cases, despatched to Messrs Robert et Antoine Garvay, Rouen, on March 26 1792, for shipment to the order of Messrs Skinner and Fenwick of Bordeaux, to friends of theirs in Philadelphia. On September 3 1790, M. Moët had despatched to the same Rouen forwarding agents, and also to the order of Messrs Skinner and Fenwick, of Bordeaux, 180 bottles of Champagne packed in 5 hampers of 3 doz. each, for shipment to Bilbao. On September 11 1790, he despatched to a M. Papelier of Strasbourg, 600 bottles of Champagne in 6 cases of 100 bottles, which were to be sent on to a Mr Charles Gottlieb Braunig of Warsaw. On April 10 1791, a composite case containing 41 bottles of white and 10 bottles of rosé Champagne Maréchal (the name of the vineyard); 19 bottles of Montrachet, and 30 bottles of Chambertin. This case was addressed to Messrs Bernard Fontaine et Hielscher, forwarding agents of Rouen, to be sent on to St Petersburg for a Mr Nicolas Haeseler. Three days later, on April 13 1791, M. Moët despatched a hamper containing 100 bottles of Champagne to Messrs F. Flüger & Co., of Nuremberg, via Strasbourg, to be sent on to Prague to M. de Meckel, "Conseiller de S.A. le Prince Archevêque de Prague".

CHAPTER SIX

Chaptal - Parmentier - François

THERE IS NO BETTER ACCOUNT OF what the vineyards and the wines of Champagne were at the beginning of the nineteenth century than that given by Jullien in his *Topographie de tous les vignobles connus*, a very good translation of which was published in London in 1824.

"*De la Marne*. The wines are the principal riches of this department and the object of considerable commerce with all France and foreign countries. The vineyards occupy about 20,000 hectares (50,000 acres) of land and furnish, upon an average, 636,800 hectolitres (14,000,000 gallons) of wine, of which about 250,000 (5,500,000 gallons) are consumed by the inhabitants. The vine is cultivated in the five districts but it is in those of Reims and Epernay that the celebrated vineyards are found. The white wines particularly have contributed to the reputation, by their delicacy, their agreeable flavour, and perhaps still more by their sparkling *mousse*, which they preserve even in extreme age, and which, if not so highly esteemed by connoisseurs, is at least most sought after by the generality of its consumers. The *red wines* are also distinguished by much fineness, delicacy, and agreeableness . . .

"The high price of the *vins mousseux* comes not only from the quality of the wines chosen to make them, and the infinite pains required before they are finished, but also from the considerable losses, to which the proprietors and dealers are exposed in this kind of speculation, and the strange phenomoena which determine or destroy the *qualité mousseuse*. As to losses, the owners count in general upon fifteen or twenty broken in a hundred, sometimes even thirty or forty. To this must be added the diminution which takes place; as the wine is separated from the deposits by decanting, an operation which is performed at least twice.

"The phenomoena which cause or destroy the quality *mousseuse* are so surprising, that they cannot be explained. The same wine drawn the same day into bottles from the same glass house, put down in the same cellar, and placed in the same heap, mousse to such a height, and in such a division, whilst it mousses much less or not at all in another position, near such a door, or under such an air hole. Wines also, which have moussed perfectly, lose this upon the change of season. All these accidents together cause the dearness of the *vins mousseux*; they are so varied and extraordinary, that the most experienced dealers cannot foresee nor prevent them always.

"The quality of the bottles, or perhaps the degree of fire which they undergo, contribute to diminish or preserve the mousse; we are assured that this phenomoenon extends even to the drinking glasses, and that in some all the fermentation is instantly lost, whilst it is preserved in others filled at the same time."

It is quite obvious that one hundred and fifty years after the lead given by Dom Pérignon, the people of Champagne were still making sparkling wine more by guesswork than by any safe, scientific technique. None of them could have lived by sparkling wine alone; they all made and sold still red Champagne for their daily bread and sparkling wine for their butter or jam, which Jullien rightly calls "speculation".

There must have been, however, quite an improvement in the standard quality of sparkling Champagne, due to the greater use of sugar in its vinification, which was eloquently and persistently recommended by two very famous men, Chaptal and Parmentier.

Jean-Antoine Chaptal, Comte de Chanteloup, pair de France (1756-1832), was a distinguished chemist, the first to occupy the chair of Chemistry at the

Plate 5 EPLUCHAGE. The grapes are first brought to these keen-eyed women who are armed with long sharp scissors with which they remove all unsound or unripe berries, bunch by bunch.

University of Montpellier. He was *Ministre de l'Intérieur*, or Home Secretary, from 1800 to 1805, when he gave to the *préfets* of all the wine-making *départements* instructions to make the *vignerons* add sugar in the *pressoir* at the vintage time in order to raise the alcoholic strength of their wines. This is a technique which has been used ever since under the name of *chaptalisation* and has proved of great benefit in sunless years, when grapes which are not fully ripe have to be picked and pressed. Owing to their geographical position so near the northern limit beyond which grapes do not mature fully in the open, the vineyards of Champagne benefited to a greater extent than most other French vineyards from Chaptal's initiative.

Up to the advent of Napoleon and the *blocus continental*, sugar, in France, meant cane sugar, but when supplies from Martinique, Guadeloupe and other West Indian islands failed, beet-sugar took its place: it had been providentially introduced in Germany by André Sigismund Margraff (1709-1782), and to promote the culture of sugar-beet had been one of the first duties of Napoleon's Ministers of Agriculture.

Parmentier (1737-1813) did more than any other Frenchman before or since for the better feeding of the people; he was responsible for the introduction of the culture of the potato in France, and for the use of other flours than wheatflour for breadmaking, and also for the improvement in baking practices and techniques. He claimed that in France, with vineyards in four-fifths of its territory, the best source of sugar was the grape: he quoted Pliny and Virgil to show that the Romans had been accustomed to *chaptaliser* their wines some 2,000 years before Chaptal was born, whenever the sun had been sulking and the grapes were not fully ripe. They had no cane sugar and no beet sugar but they had what the French *vignerons* also had, or could easily have: sugar made from concentrated grape juice or must.[23]

Parmentier refers particularly to the *vignerons* of the Marne who would, he says, benefit more than others by adding his *sirop de raisins* in the fermenting vat at the time of the vintage.[24]

Parmentier also knew that in the past cane sugar had been added to the sharp, young *saute-bouchon* to make it more acceptable and he claimed that his *sirop de raisins* was much better than cane sugar for sweetening Champagne, as it blended with the wine more rapidly and more perfectly. "Le sirop de raisins

édulcore les vins de Champagne avec plus d'avantage que le sucre candi; c'est une vérité trop palpable pour pouvoir être révoquée en doute. Mais ce qui lui donne un nouveau mérite c'est que . . . au bout de 48 heures le vin est d'une limpidité étonnante et que sa liqueur est aussi belle que si elle avait été filtrée." [25]

In a letter which he wrote in August 1801 from Epernay to M. Cadet-Devaux, Nicolas Perrier remarks that formerly sugar was added to sharp wines to make them more acceptable and that it was added after the wine had finished fermenting, whereas the new technique – Chaptal's – consisted in adding sugar in the fermenting vat, and it improved the wines so much that the price of the second class wines of Ay, commonly called *vins de vignerons*, had risen in a manner never heard of before. [45]

The French Revolution had swept away the gay Marquis and the wise monks of Sillery and Hautvillers, and many changes had taken place, for better or worse, in the ownership of famous Champagne vineyards. Jullien refers to some of those changes: "Before the Revolution, the Seigneur of this Domain (Sillery) possessed upon the declivities of Verzenay, Mailly and Ludes, a great extent of excellent vines, furnishing wine of the same kind and of equal reputation with those of Sillery. The most part of those has been sold to rich proprietors who still cultivate them with the same care. The wine of Sillery is less sought after in France than in foreign countries; it is particularly esteemed in England . . ."

"Hautvillers, four leagues from Reims, furnished formerly wines which equalled or surpassed those of Ay: but many of the vineyards, having fallen into the hands of persons who do not cultivate them with the same care, their produce, though good, is placed in the second class only." [30]

In the 1816 edition of his *Topographie de tous les vignobles connus*, Jullien gives 14 million gallons as the Marne production, and 5,300,000 bottles as the quantity of sparkling Champagne made; in the 1848 edition, he gives 15,400,000 gallons as the total production of the Marne, and 5,500,000 bottles as the sparkling wine figure.

During the reign of Napoleon, and for some years after, sparkling Champagne represented only a third of the wines of the Marne vineyards. Jullien says quite definitely that the *mousse pétillante* had a great appeal for *la foule des amateurs* and mostly those of foreign lands, but that it was by no means what the *vrais gourmets* esteemed most in the wines of Champagne.[28]

Thanks to Chaptal and Parmentier, sparkling Champagne, during the first half of the nineteenth century, was no longer the "green" wine which it was during the eighteenth century, whenever the sun failed to co-operate, as happened only too often. But sugar, without any reliable means of control, meant a greater number of burst bottles, and breakages, or *la casse*, were a constant nightmare for the Champagne shippers. The sediment – *le dépôt* – which fouled the look of the undecanted wine, was also one of their worst headaches. Decanting a sparkling wine is a difficult and wasteful operation, and the *dégorgement*, the gathering of the sediment upon the inside face of the cork before letting it fly out with the released cork, was not known until the

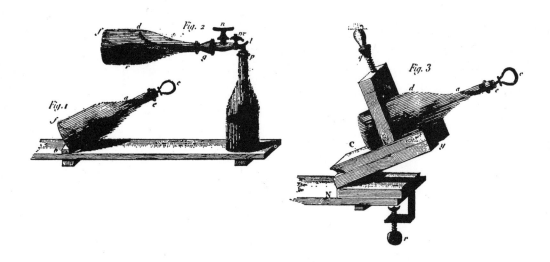

opening years of the nineteenth century. It was first described by Jullien in 1813.[26] After being either *décantées* or *dégorgées* – and sometimes they were both decanted and "disgorged" – the bottles had to be filled up; no easy task, indeed, to pour sparkling wine into sparkling wine! One gets a fair idea of the trouble people took to get sparkling Champagne free from all sediment if one studies the different gadgets used at the time as depicted in the folding plate of Jullien's *Manuel du Sommelier*, some of which are reproduced above.

But it was *la casse*, or breakages – seldom less than 10 % of a *tirage* or bottling and sometimes as much as 80 % – which was responsible for the high cost of sparkling Champagne and for the highly speculative nature of the Champagne trade. What made matters even worse was the fact that the wines of the sunnier summers – and riper grapes – invariably suffered most: this was not surprising since they were richer in sugar. Of course, ever since Dom Pérignon, it had been known that the sweeter the grapes the more alcohol and carbonic acid gas there will be in the wine; the problem which had to be solved was how to gauge the quantity of sugar in a wine before it was bottled and safely corked. One wine might contain more sugar than another and yet *taste* less sweet, if

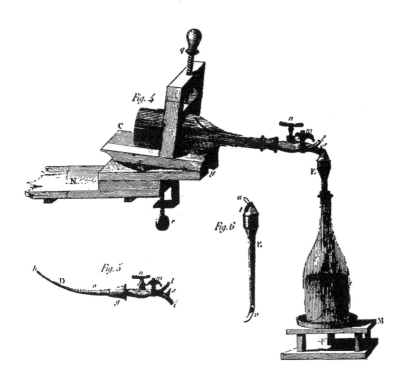

it had a higher proportion of acidity, the effect of the acidity being to hide the sugar content. It was not until 1836 that a *pharmacien* of Châlons-sur-Marne, François, published his *Nouvelles observations sur la fermentation de vin en bouteilles, suivies d'un procédé pour reconnaître la quantité de sucre contenu dans le vin immédiatement avant le tirage.*

At about the same time a *professeur de mathématiques*, Monsieur de Maizières, invented a gadget, which he called *paracasse*, to prevent the bursting of Champagne bottles, but it did not prove to be of any use. No description or drawing of it appears to be available. François, on the other hand, was responsible for placing the Champagne trade upon a sound economic footing by his method, which was known at the time as *réduction François*, or *dosage* for measuring sugar. Henceforth it became possible to find out exactly how much sugar there was in a wine before it was bottled and to add to it, when necessary, the quantity of sugar corresponding to the exact volume of carbonic acid gas wanted: for a moderately sparkling wine, a pressure corresponding to 4½ or 5 *atmosphères*, and from 5 to 6 *atmosphères* for a *grand mousseux* that will shoot its cork to the ceiling.

Strangely enough, François's *procédé* was not accepted immediately by all in the Champagne country, but it was hailed with the greatest enthusiasm wherever else grapes grew, for henceforth wine could be made sparkling with a fair measure of certainty.

"Until the first years of the nineteenth century, the Département de la Marne was the only country where sparkling wine was made but there are now sparkling wines made in a number of other places. But none of those wines, in our opinion, possesses any of the qualities which distinguish the *véritable vin de Champagne*. What figure can possibly have next to the wines of Ay, Reims and Epernay, the wine of Arbois, *véritable casse-tête*, Limoux, Bergerac, Sauternes, *misérables parodies*, unworthy of the refined palates of *fins gourmets*." [35]

Burgundy had challenged the Champagne monopoly as early as 1820, when a Monsieur J. Laussère, of Nuits St-Georges, first made sparkling Burgundy, producing 150,000 bottles in 1820, and a million bottles in each of the years 1825, 1826 and 1827.

Then came the sparkling wines of Arbois, Saumur, Vouvray, and St-Péray; then Switzerland, the Moselle and the Rhine; Württemberg, Saxony, Silesia brought forth sparkling wines of Esslingen, Dresden and Grüneberg! So far so good; they are within their rights. Champagne has nothing to fear from all such imitations so long as they do not, as some have dared to do, take the name of Champagne, in order to improve their chances of selling their wines! [36] Evidently Max Sutaine had not heard of sparkling Catawba, and we can well imagine his indignation if he had seen the New York Astor House wine list for 1839 quoting an anonymous "Sparkling Hock" at three dollars per bottle, and an anonymous "Côte d'Or" at one dollar and fifty cents per pint, while Clicquot and Perrier-Jouët were quoted at two dollars per bottle and one dollar per pint.

Thanks to François, the making of sparkling wine soon became a less hazardous undertaking than in the past, so that the Champagne shippers were able to offer their wines at much lower prices than before. And wine-merchants, not only in France, but in Switzerland, England and elsewhere, could and did sell Champagne to the public at prices likely to appeal to a far larger number of consumers. Here are a few pre-François and post-François Champagne quotations which illustrate the difference in Champagne prices:

Johann Wichelhausen, Zurich. 1819 Price List:

Champagne mousseux No. 1	2 Fl.45 per single bott.	2 Fl.38 per bott. per doz.
Champagne mousseux No. 2	2 Fl.10 ,, ,, ,,	2 Fl. 8 per bott. per doz.
Œil de perdrix mousseux No. 1	2 Fl. ,, ,, ,,	
Œil de perdrix mousseux No. 2	2 Fl.30 ,, ,, ,,	2 Fl.10 per bott. per doz.

Klauser Meyer, Zurich. 1821 Price List:

Champagner moussirend	2 Fl. per bottle
Œil de perdrix	2 Fl. ,, ,,

The London Wine Company. 1823 Circular:

Champagne, white sparkling from £4.10.0. to £7.7.0. per dozen bottles	
Champagne creaming	£5. 5.0. to £7.7.0. ,, ,, ,,
Champagne pink	£5. 5.0. to £7.7.0. ,, ,, ,,

(These were retail price.)

> Charles Wright, Wine Merchant to His R.H. the Duke of Clarence, next to the King's and opposite the Haymarket Theatre, Opera Colonnade, London, is now landing *Champagne*, ROUGE ET BLANC, First Quality, brillant condition (G.Prix Soleau Avize, growers) 41.4s. per doz... (Front page advertisement in the *British Mercury and Wednesday Evening Post.* Wednesday, May 28, 1823.)

James Barry, 16 Mincing Lane. 1825 Circular:

Champagne, best quality	95s. to 100s. per dozen bottles
Champagne, pink, creaming	95s. to 100s. ,, ,, ,,
Champagne, Sillery	90s. to 100 s. ,, ,, ,,

(These were wholesale prices to the trade.)

In their Circular dated August 20, 1829, Quarles Harris of 41 Crutched Friars quoted as follows:

Finest Champagne, White and Pink, Creaming   70s.
,,   ,,   ,,   ,,   ,, Sparkling   70s.
,,   ,,   Brown and Vin d'Ay   80s.

The next item is Burgundy   110s.

In 1830, one of the smart wine merchants of Paris, with a shop in the Rue du Mail and another in the Passage de Choiseul, offered the following varieties of Champagne:

Sillery	5.00 francs
Château Ai	5.50
Château Ai rosé	4.50
Château Epernay	3.50
Château Epernay rosé	3.50
Tisane	2.00

In London, at about the same time: D. Watts, of the St Marylebone wine and spirit Depot, 48 Chapel Street, Edgware Road, "begs to submit the following prices for the instruction of the public, assuring them that a saving of at least six shillings per dozen is made by purchasing wine at this establishment, the business being conducted entirely for ready money; consequently he is enabled to offer wines and spirits of the choicest quality on very advantageous terms."

Champagne good quality	60s. and 66s.
Champagne Moët's, first quality	80s.

(An advertisement in *The Town, c. 1830*.)

Joseph Seebie, wine-merchant, whose shop stood at the corner of Marlborough and Tyler Streets, near the top of Regent Street, London, sent out a Circular offering Champagne at from 58s. to 86s. per dozen.

Matthew Clark & Keeling, 72 Great Tower Street. 1838 & 1839, Circulars:
Champagne First Quality 40s. to 50s. per doz. duty paid delivered in London
Champagne Good Quality
    and other qualities   22s. to 36s. ,,   ,,   duty paid delivered in London

(These were wholesale prices to the Trade.)

John G.Oliver, Bury St Edmunds. Invoice dated June 21, 1843

Sparkling Champagne	50s. per Dozen bottles
Sparkling Hock	60s. per Dozen bottles
Lafite & Margaux	69s. per Dozen bottles

On July 7, 1849, John Worlledge wrote to Seymour & Sons, in whose Circular Champagne was quoted at from 58s. to 84s., as follows: "I will thank you to forward me a 3 doz. case of the best Champagne as usual at 64s. per doz."

A decade later, in 1858, Barraclough, Pellatt & Muspratt of 107 Upper Thames Street and 39 King William Street, London Bridge, still offered "Champagne 54s. to 84s. per doz.", while they quoted Claret at from 33s. to 100s., and Hock and Moselle at from 48s. to 96s., and Superior Pale Cognac at from 32s. to 36s. per gallon.

Two years later, in 1860, the London Foreign Vineyards Association Ltd was offering the following sparkling wines:

The celebrated Epernay, 1848 vintage	40s. per dozen
Imperial Sillery de Palais	48s.
Moët & Chandon 1st growth 1846	60s.
Perrier Jouët 1st growth	60s.
Mumm's 1st growth	60s.
Giesler	60s.
Mde Clicquot's à la Russe	60s.
E.Clicquot's dry Sillery	58s.
Ai Royal Fleur de Sillery mousseux	54s.
Choice rare Sillery sec (non-mousseux)	84s.
Sparkling White Fleur de Haute Bourgogne	42s.
Finest sparkling Moselle or Hock	44s. and 52s.

According to Cyrus Redding,[37] the total quantity of wine made in the Marne *département* in 1832, was 480,000 hectolitres (10,560,000 gallons), of which 310,000 hectolitres (6,820,000 gallons) were red beverage wines of the *ordinaire* class, fit for local consumption only; 120,000 hectolitres (2,640,000 gallons) of 'quality' red wines, and 50,000 hectolitres (1,100,000 gallons) of white wines suitable for making sparkling Champagne. This would mean, if Reddings' figures are reliable, that all the sparkling Champagne of 1832, one of the best vintages of the nineteenth century, amounted to not much over one million gallons, some 6,600,000 bottles in all. And, still according to Cyrus Redding, the more important markets for the sale of sparkling Champagne were at the time as follows:

France	626,000 bottles
Germany	479,000
England and India	467,000
U.S.A.	400,000
Sweden and Denmark	30,000

It was only from the forties onwards that the demand for the still red wines of Champagne declined to vanishing point, whilst the trade in sparkling Champagne really got into its stride, many more people becoming Champagne shippers after François had made the business so much less hazardous. From 1844 to 1869, France had recovered from the ruinous drain on men and treasure of the Napoleonic wars, and the bulk of the population was little affected by the changes of regimes – the end of the long line of kings when Louis-Philippe abdicated, the short-lived Second Republic, and the brilliant reign of Napoleon III that ended so disastrously in 1870. During those twenty-five years, the sales of Champagne in France remained steady, rising slowly from 2,255,438 bottles to 3,628,401 bottles, a rise of 61 %. During the same period, the quantity of Champagne exported rose from 4,380,214 bottles to 13,858,830 bottles, a rise of 216.4 %. The United Kingdom and the United States were chiefly responsible for this sensational increase. It was during that time that the Industrial Revolution transformed the population of a chiefly agricultural England into an urban one, more and more goods being made to sell, and less and less food being grown to eat, resulting in greater prosperity and affluence than had ever been known before.

CHAPTER SEVEN

Champagne and Sugar

I N SPITE OF PARMENTIER'S EXPERIMENTS and his eloquent appeal
to the *vignerons* to use *sirop de raisins* rather than sugar to sweeten sparkling
Champagne, sugar won, and when François's *densimètre* had at long last
beaten the disastrous *casse* in the forties and fifties of the nineteenth century,
there was cheap sparkling Champagne for everyone – or nearly everyone –
and it was sweet wine, most of it very young and very sweet.

The place of any sweet wine at mealtime is at the end of the meal, with the
sweets or dessert, and this was the place given to sparkling Champagne in
France from the outset, a place which it held for a hundred years – that is, until
the Second World War. It replaced the Lunel, Banyuls, Frontignan, Grenache
and other *vins doux naturels* of the South, the traditional *vins de dessert*. In England, however, the traditional after-dinner wines, Port, Sherry and Madeira,
had much deeper roots in the hearts or rather the palates of wine drinkers.
Port, of course, was by far the most popular of the three and there had never
been finer wines than the Port vintages of 1834, 1840, 1842 and 1847, far greater
wines these than any of the sweet wines of the Languedoc. There could not
be any question of serving Champagne at the end of the meal instead of or as

an alternative to Port. Its place was either before or at the beginning of the meal, with fish or white meat. As early as 1835 Thomas Walker, describing a dinner ordered at Lovegrove's Restaurant at Blackwall on August 12, wrote:

"With the turtle, of course, there will be punch; with the whitebait Champagne; with the grouse Claret; the two former I have ordered to be particularly well iced, and they will be placed in succession on the table, so that we can all help ourselves."

Incidentally, Thomas Walker very rightly maintained that it was better not to have Champagne at all rather than to "dole it out like drops of blood". [38]

At another dinner at the same place a few months later: "Our party consisted of four. We had, I think, a bottle of Sherry only, two or three bottles (I forget which) of Champagne, one of Sauterne, and two of us drank Port, and two Claret after dinner." (*The Quarterly Review*. February 1836.)

Obviously, very sweet Champagne would not have been acceptable with food, and the very sweet wines were those of the poorer vintages which were sold when very young, whereas the wines of the better vintages were kept longer and were not so "richly" liqueured. They were the wines which have been known ever since as vintage Champagne, sold under the date of their vintage, but they were then sweeter than vintage Champagne of the present day. It is remarkable how long those early vintage Champagnes could be kept and still retain their appeal for the connoisseurs of old, as evidenced by the prices which they fetched at public auctions at Christie's:

    1842 Mumm fetched 62s. per dozen bottles in 1855;
    1842 Moët fetched 55s. in 1871;
    1846 Perrier-Jouët First Quality fetched from 55s. to 57s. in 1857;
    1846 Louis Roederer fetched 44s. in 1859;
    1846 Clicquot fetched 86s. in 1871;
    1857 Cliquot fetched 90s. in 1865;
    1857 Moët fetched 67s. in 1871;
    1857 Perrier-Jouët fetched 49s. in 1861 and 65s. in 1864.

This last wine, Perrier-Jouët 1857, which Professor George Saintsbury drank in 1884, was not only still fit to drink, then 27 years old, but the Professor considered that it was the best Champagne he ever tasted: "It was supposed to have formed part of a parcel originally shipped for Queen Victoria and designated 't.c.', that is to say *très coloré*. When I bought it in May 1884 it was twenty-seven years old, of a deep amber colour, and nearly but not quite still, though not at all ullaged. It was so majestical that one was inclined to leave it quite alone and to drink it like a slightly sparkling liqueur." [58]

"Majestical" Champagne belonged to the age of the crinoline, not of the bikini!

I was a very young man when Mr Barwell, of Norwich, an elderly gentleman, told me that he had first been to Champagne to buy wine for his firm in 1842, and that he had bought a very good wine at Ay for 16s. per dozen bottles, in bin. This and other Champagnes which he had bought during his long life were sold by his firm as Barwell No. 1 and Barwell No. 2, the name of the French shipper never being disclosed. This was the practice of many firms in England until the sixties and there was good reason for it, since many English wine-merchants often shipped Champagne of their own choice, which were drier than the standard wines shipped under the name or brand of the shippers from whom they had secured their wines.

Mr Burne, for instance, the senior of Messrs Burne, Turner & Co., one of the pioneers of Dry Champagne, when at Epernay, in 1848, tasted one of Perrier-Jouët's 1846 *cuvées* in its *brut* – unliqueured – state, and he liked it so much that he begged M. Charles Perrier to let him have some that would be only slightly liqueured: M. Perrier did his best to dissuade him, convinced as he was that a dry Champagne would not be to the taste of the public; in the end, however, he agreed to ship to Mr Burne a small quantity as an experiment. When Mr Burne got this dry Champagne, bearing his own firm's name, not that of Perrier–Jouët, he sold it to a London military club, but the "Boys" found it so "awfully" dry that the enterprising wine-merchant had the mortification of having to take it back and replace it with a sweeter wine.

Nothing daunted, however, Mr Burne asked M. Louis Roederer, in 1850, to let him have some *brut* Champagne; he flatly refused, but Mr Burne managed to get some dry Champagne from another firm: other English wine-merchants did the same, so that by the end of the 'fifties and during the 'sixties, quite a number of the Reims, Ay and Epernay firms sold "English *cuvées*" with much less sweetness than the *cuvées* which they sold in France and elsewhere on the Continent. Both Clicquot and Heidsieck shipped an 1857 Vintage *cuvée* that was labelled "Dry"; Bollinger shipped a "Very Dry" 1865 Vintage; and Ayala also shipped a "Very Dry" 1865 vintage, which became very popular at Oxford, chiefly on account of the favour which it enjoyed at the Bullingdon Club, where the then Prince of Wales occasionally met his college friends.

The next good Champagne vintage, after 1865, was the 1868 which was shipped by many of the leading shippers as "Dry", or "Very Dry" or "Extra Sec", at from 2s. to 6s. more per dozen bottles than the 1865's.

One of the consequences of selling much drier Champagne to England was that it appreciated rapidly in quality and value with age. Thus at Christie's in 1875, 140s. per dozen bottles was the price paid for Perrier-Jouët Extra Dry 1868 and 122s. for Pommery Extra Sec 1868, whilst the highly sugared Clicquot "Rich" at the same sale merely fetched 65s.

It was really during the 'seventies that the cult of sugared Champagne slowly but surely came to an end. There were to the last, particularly in the provinces, old "connoisseurs" who were faithful to sweet wines as long as these were obtainable. Thus Messrs Barwell, of Norwich and London, were still importing fairly sweet Champagne for their Norwich clientèle long after they sold none but dry Champagne in London. As late as 1868 Messrs Chavasse of Birmingham imported some George Goulet with 16 % sugar!

Eventually the champions of sugar were outnumbered by a host of new recruits who had never tasted the outmoded sweet wines. The change is thus recorded by Professor Saintsbury in his *Notes on a Cellar Book*:

"However, the change came, and it was not finally accomplished when my Cellar Book was started. The head of the great House of Roederer was, even later, said to have declared that as long as *he* lived there should be no bowing to the dry Baal of his cellars; and, at any rate in the country, Clicquot was more often still sweet – not to the 'Russe' extent, which was only good for savages or children, but yet not dry."

The wines of 1870 were quite good but by no means plentiful; yet they were cheap owing to the Franco-Prussian war and political unrest in France. The next three vintages, 1871, 1872 and 1873, were bad ones – 1873 the worst of them – and to make matters worse the Champagne country was occupied by the Germans as bail for the payment of the war "indemnity". With ruin staring them in the face, the Champagne shippers were obliged to raise their prices for the wines they could still offer at a time when their stocks were at the lowest ebb; even then, the best brands of Champagne did not cost more than from 66s. to 75s. per dozen bottles, duty paid, London.

Happily, the vintage of 1874 proved to be a magnificent one: the grapes, however, were so ripe when picked and pressed that their wines were of a distinctly darker shade of gold than usual and most of them also had a pinkish sheen which made it easy to tell a '74 Champagne at first sight. All firms shipped some of their '74's as *Brut* or Extra Dry and it may rightly be said that this vintage settled definitely, as far as England was concerned, any controversy as to the relative merits of sweet and dry Champagne in favour of the latter.

The popularity of the 1874 Champagnes was something quite unheard of in England or anywhere else and it introduced an element of speculation which lasted for the best part of fifty years. Madame Pommery's *Brut* 1874, for instance, was sold at 71s. per dozen bottles, f.o.b., in 1880; its market (wholesale) price in April 1882 was 110s.; at Christie's, five years later, the same wine fetched 270s. per dozen (*The Wine Trade Review*. April 15, 1882.) Such a sensational appreciation in so short a time created an unprecedented demand for the more popular brands: they were not, of course, recognized as Trustees' Stock, but many considered them an excellent investment. In 1895, when past its best and showing unmistakeable signs of approaching decay, Pommery 1874 still fetched 200s. per dozen at public sales; also it received the unusual compliment of a "Farewell" ode in December 1894:

ODE TO POMMERY 1874

Air: Old Lang Syne

Should auld acquaintance be forgot
'Twixt human friends and wine?
Nay, for do both most surely not
Bring back the "Auld Lang Syne"?

Here's to their cork a tender hand,
It's wanted now, old friend;
Nor screw, nor nippers will thou stand,
Thou'rt still and near thy end.

We twa hae met o'er snowy cloth
Ofttimes midst crystal fine;
Now dubious drinks, with fizzy froth,
Replace the "Auld Lang Syne".

Then reverently knock the wax
From off thy ancient strings;
Alas! thy cork shows divers cracks,
Thy flavour, has it wings?

Ah no! my trusted friend;
Thy colour has not paled;
Like Statesman drawing near his end,
The froth, not strength, has failed.

Farewell, then, Pommery Seventy-Four!
With reverential sips
We part and grieve that never more
Such wine may pass our lips.

RICHARD JOHN LLOYD PRICE
Vanity Fair. December 27 1894

Plate 6 PRESSOIR. The square press which is filled to the brim
with ripe grapes: the lid of great oak beams will then be dropped
on them and driven down by a central screw. The juice crushed
out of the grapes will run out through the wooden fence round
the four sides of the *pressoir*.

In France, where Champagne was still the sweet *vin de dessert*, its sales in 1890 were just about the same as in 1850, whilst in England, where Champagne had become the *vin de table de luxe*, a dry wine that one could enjoy before and during meals, sales rose from an average of 3,000,000 bottles per annum during the 'sixties to an average of 9,000,000 bottles per annum during the 'eighties and 'nineties. Of course, there were some "well-informed" persons who would from time to time let it be known that there was not nearly enough wine made in the Champagne country to keep pace with the increased demand, so that there were now fields of rhubarb in Yorkshire that kept up the necessary supply of juicy stalks from which the Champagne shippers made some of their wines. And there were people who accepted this utter nonsense at its face value. Of course, the "well-informed" persons had overlooked the fact that whilst the export of Champagne had trebled in less than thirty years, when the number of Champagne vineyards and their output of wine had hardly changed at all, the proportion of still wines made in the Marne during the 'sixties was much greater than that of the sparkling wines; thirty years later, the situation was reversed. It is only too true that, after three consecutive bad vintages – 1871, 1872 and 1873 – stocks of sparkling Champagne were alarmingly low, but matters were soon righted by three large consecutive vintages – 1874, 1875 and 1876. After 1874, which brought forth a great deal of wine of superlative quality, came 1875 – the most abundant vintage of the century, a very fair proportion of its wines being of very good quality: those two years provided a sufficient quantity of good vintage wines suitable for export for four or five years to come. Then came 1876, when a large quantity of wine was again vintaged, wine of very poor quality but very inexpensive and with plenty of sugar added, good enough for sale in France.

The popularity of the drier – and better – wines in England, which was to a great extent responsible for the prosperity of the Champagne trade, was due to the keen competition existing between Champagne shippers and the very low prices at which Champagne of quite good quality could be bought.

There were during the last decade of the nineteenth century more than twice the number of Champagne shippers than there are today, perhaps even three times as many, and most of them worked very hard to make their brands or their own names known, which added up to a great deal of propaganda for

Champagne. As regards prices, comparisons with those of today are not so much odious as ridiculous. Thus, in 1880, after the total failure of the 1879 vintage, the smallest of the century, all the shippers were compelled to raise their prices. These are the prices they charged – wholesale prices, of course – to importers who distributed the wines to retailers in England:

Ayala	45s., 55s. and 65s. per doz. f.o.r. Ay.
Bollinger	65s. per doz. f.o.b.
Delbeck	38s., 48s. and 58s. per doz. f.o.r. Reims.
Giesler	40s., 56s., 66s. per doz. f.o.b.
Geo. Goulet	64s. per doz. f.o.b.
Krug	63s. and 65s. per doz. f.o.b.
G.H.Mumm	60s., 64s., 68s. per doz. f.o.b.
Perrier-Jouët	24s., 34s., 54s,. 64s. per doz. in bin Epernay.
	62s. & 72s. per doz. duty paid, delivered London.
Pfungst	62s., 62s., 64s., 72s. per doz. f.o.r. Epernay
H.Piper	68s. per doz. in bond London.
Pol Roger	56s. per doz. in bin Epernay.
Ruinart	58s., 66s., 72s. per doz. f.o.b. Dry Sillery 94s.
St-Marceaux	56s., 66s., 72s. per doz. in bond London.

Exceptionally low as these prices may appear to us today, they were higher than they had ever been before. Only a dozen years earlier, in his 1867 Circular, A. Hubinet, Madame Pommery's agent in London, was offering to the trade a "Fine Quality (Dry) Pommery" at 46s. per dozen bottles duty. paid, London, and the choice of either the "Carte Blanche Medium Dry" or the "Carte Blanche Very Dry" at 56s. per dozen bottles, and 60s. per two dozen half-bottles, duty paid, London. At the same time, he announced that he had made arrangements with a shipper of "Cheap Champagnes" and that he could recommend as being natural wines, fit for keeping, a Medium Dry Pale Champagne at 16s. f.o.b. (24s. duty paid), and another at 24s. f.o.b. (32s. duty paid).

Those were the days when Champagne cost but 5s. at the Union Club and 6s. at the Bodega – for a single bottle; 5s. 6d. per bottle for a dozen; and when responsible, sober people, like W. E. Gladstone, considered that a bottle of Champagne for dinner was a reasonable allowance for a gentleman.

CHAPTER EIGHT

The Golden Age

THERE NEVER HAD BEEN MORE nor better wines made in Champagne than were made during the twenty years from 1889 to 1908, and although much good Champagne was made during the fifty years from 1911 to 1960, there has not been any quite comparable in excellence to the best *cuvées* of 1889, 1892, 1899, 1900, 1904 and 1906. But if the two decades between 1889-1908 deserve to be called the Golden Age of Champagne, it is mainly because during that period the people of Champagne enjoyed a measure of prosperity undreamt of by their predecessors and unknown to their successors. Yet, strange to say, it was during this "Golden Age" that the Champagne vineyards fell a prey to the *Phylloxera vastatrix*.

Champagne fared much better than Bordeaux, where the vineyards were destroyed with quite staggering rapidity. The accursed little vine louse, the *Phylloxera vastatrix*, was noticed for the first time in Champagne at Tréloup, a hamlet on the borders of the Aisne and Marne *départements*, in 1890, that is, twelve years after the Bordeaux vineyards were hit. But by 1892, there were 5 acres of vineyards in the Marne reported as having been "invaded" by the enemy; in 1894 there were 12 acres and 35 acres in 1897. Owing to the colder weather and other climatic factors, the phylloxera made slow progress at first in the Champagne vineyards, and the Champenois also had the benefit of knowing what had been done by the Bordelais to fight the invader: in the Gironde, they had been caught untirely unprepared; the people of Champagne were not. A meeting of all the *vignerons* was called at Epernay by the Préfet on June 13, 1891, and all were asked to unite and help fight the dreaded pest at their door. Had the *vignerons* responded as they should have done, the vineyards of Champagne might have been saved, but out of a total of 25,729 proprietors of vineyards who owned 32,053 acres, 17,370 who owned 24,425 acres joined the newly formed *Syndicat de Défense*, and 12,821 who owned 7,627 acres, refused to do so. They were mostly small-holders, and they not only declined to pay a single *sou* to buy the *sulfure de carbone* so badly needed to fight the pest, but they went out of their way to make it more difficult or even impossible for their more intelligent neighbours to carry on the fight. But the fight went on, a losing fight of course, yet by no means a hopeless one since it retarded the inroads of the bug and gave time to replant vineyards with grafted vines, year by year, where the original French vines had to be up-rooted.

The following figures show the rate of progress of the phylloxera in the Marne.[63] In 1897, 35 acres were affected; in 1898, 100 acres; in 1899, 250 acres; in 1900, 1,650 acres; in 1901, 3,000 acres; in 1902, 5,000 acres, in 1903, 5,000 acres; in 1904, 6,000 acres; in 1905, 8,000 acres; in 1906, 10,000 acres; in 1907, 12,000 acres; in 1908, 14,000 acres; in 1909, 15,000 acres, and in 1910, 16,000 acres, or pretty well exactly half the vineyards of the Marne.

During those 20 years, motoring came of age and aviation was born; incidentally it was with Champagne and in Champagne that aviation was christened, at *La Grande Semaine d'Aviation de Reims*, the first of all international aviation meetings or displays, at Bétheny, from August 22 to 29, 1909. Ever since, the faster and more restless tempo of living has proved fatal to leisure and to the enjoyment of after-dinner Port, but it has not diminished the popularity of Champagne in the least: quite the contrary!

It was also during those same 20 years that a social revolution took place which benefited Champagne. There had been up to that time two very different sorts of "smart" women in London, Paris, New York, and other great cities: those whose heart's desire – and profession or vocation – was to please men;

and the others: they did not mix. It was only in the late 'eighties, with César Ritz at the Savoy and Bertini in the Criterion's East Room, that a new and much higher standard of elegance and refinement was introduced into the catering world: for the first time *grand luxe* and *bon goût* were happily partnered, and for the first time also the wives, sisters and daughters of members of the old

aristocracy and of captains of industry or of wealthy financiers dined with their male escorts in fashionable public places, where they had no objection whatever – far from it! – to meeting all the more glamorous *cocottes* of the day, a species that became extinct when easy divorces came in. And, of course, Champagne was *de rigueur* in all smart hotels and restaurants, with the exception perhaps of the Café Royal: there they had a cellar of great Clarets and Burgundies unobtainable elsewhere, whereas there was a wonderful choice of excellent Champagne vintages, most reasonably priced, from the 1874s, for those who liked old Champagne, to the wines of 1880, 1884 and 1889. The 1889s were particularly delicious from the start, when still quite young, and they retained their charm for many years.

One of the great privileges which Champagne shippers have now lost, one which was a great asset to them during the "Golden Age", was the liberty which all enjoyed – and a few, alas, abused – to make up their *cuvées* as they thought best. In 1889, for instance, there was not much wine made, owing to late spring frosts, but the summer was so wonderful that the quality of the wine of that year was exceptionally fine, so much so that the bidding for whatever grapes the *vignerons* had to sell was very keen, and prices rocketed to heights unheard of at the time, that is for the grapes of all the best vineyards. Happily, there were also grapes to be had at a fraction of the price in other vineyards which had escaped the spring frosts, although not so very far from those of the Marne, in the nearby Aube and Aisne *départements*. They, too, had benefited by the wonderful summer of 1889. Their grapes were sound but the wines which were made from them were much lighter than those of the Marne; yet they were quite nice little wines. They were bought by the Reims and Epernay firms, who were free to do so then – they could not do so today – and blended with the big, rather too big, wines of the *grands crus*. This not only reduced appreciably the original cost price of the 1889 *cuvées*, but it also improved their quality, giving them a measure of lightness which they would not have had otherwise.

The 'nineties, the "Gay Nineties" as they were dubbed in England, were perhaps the most wonderful decade of the "Golden Age". There was peace in the world and plenty at home; labour was very cheap and so were the grapes, most of them good grapes, particularly in Champagne; profits had never been greater nor prospects happier at Reims and Epernay, and also in Paris and London, New York and Buenos Aires, Moscow and Vienna. The demand for Champagne increased in France, where the wine was still the sweet dessert wine which people merely sipped, but it did not increase at anything like the same ratio as it did abroad, particularly in the United Kingdom and the United States, where people did not sip but drank dry Champagne as a table wine *de luxe*.

The two best vintages of the 'nineties were those of 1892 and 1899 as regards quality, but the most remarkable vintage of the decade was 1893. The heat of the summer was so great and lasted so long that many wells dried up and there was a great shortage of water, so much so that, at the time of the vintage, at Cramant, anybody with a horse, a cart and an empty cask, who would go to the Marne and deliver at the *pressoir* a cask of Marne water to wash and cool the presses, could go home with his cask full of new wine in exchange, no money passing: water was as valuable as wine. There was so much wine made in 1893, and it was so good at first, that a number of new firms started in that year and the next, whilst all the older firms piled up reserves of wines of the best growths to be used in coming years, to raise the quality of poor quality vintages and to lower the cost of good ones. Unfortunately, delicious as the 93s were when very young, they grew dark in colour with age, and rather coarse as well; they were not well balanced; they lacked acidity and although they did help to lower the price of later vintages with which they were blended, they did not better them as much as had been expected.

There was some good wine made in 1895, but many of the 1895 *cuvées* gave a good deal of trouble to the shippers: they threw a "blue smoke" sediment which did not affect the taste of the wine but fouled its good looks. Of course, a shipper is responsible for the wine that bears his name or brand from the moment he sells it until the wine is drunk, so that shippers offered to take back from their customers and replace with perfectly clear bottles any of those that had become cloudy after a while. There was but one restaurateur, in London, to my own knowledge, who never complained and who would not hear of returning and exchanging any of the '95s he had bought: Oscar Philippe. He hailed from Luxembourg and owned the Cavour in Leicester Square. He listed his '95s as "clear" and "thick", and he sold them all in no time without, he told me, anybody ever lodging a complaint.

There was a fairly large quantity of wine made in 1896, none of which was of fine quality, but all or most of it was sound enough and most useful for the making of non-vintage *cuvées* with the help of 1893 reserves.

In 1897, there was much less wine than in 1896, but it was of distinctly better quality, although not nearly good enough for the vintage Champagne standard of those days.

In 1898, the quantity of wine made was well above the average, and most of the wine was of very fair quality. It could easily have been shipped as a vintage of the 1953 standard, and it was shipped as a vintage by some of the Champagne shippers: others did not do so because the next two vintages, 1899 and 1900, proved to be so much better, and they did not wish, as a matter of policy, to ship three consecutive years as vintages.

The '99s were better wines, but there was never enough of them. The vintage was too small for the demand and the wines were drunk too quickly. Those that were kept and given a chance to show how good they could be proved admirable: I can vouch for this since I was privileged to enjoy some '99 that was absolutely perfect when twenty-five years old.

In 1900, happily, the vineyards of Champagne brought forth not only very good wines but an abundance of them; they were also very much cheaper to buy at the vintage time than the grapes or new wines of the previous vintage. One franc per kilog. was the price paid for the most magnificent wine-making grapes I ever saw, perfectly sound and ripe. The 1900s were no better than the '99s, but they were very good, rather smoother, softer, and sooner ready to drink. Most people at the time supposed that it would be better to drink the 1900s and keep the '99s, as the younger wines were not likely to last the so well. But the 1900's did last for a very long time and as there were a great many more 1900s than '99s, they were given a better chance to show how well they could stand the test of age. The most difficult test I ever gave a 1900 was when we opened three magnums of Champagne at home for a party of Champagne-loving friends in July, 1931: there was a magnum of 1906, one of 1904 and one of 1900, all three from the same shipper, and in the voting the 1904 and 1900 were given equal votes for the first place; the 1904 was the better wine, the fresher wine, we agreed, but there was something in the "farewell" of the 1900 that was more lingering and quite fascinating – in spite of the thirty years the wine had spent in solitary confinement!

From 1900 to 1908, much Champagne was made, and most of it was of fair, fine or superlative quality: the best being the wines of 1904 and 1906, whilst the 1905, 1907 and 1908 vintages were all good though not nearly as good.

The vintage of 1910 was one of the worst on record. It heralded a chapter of troubles, a new era. The "Golden Age" had come to an end.

During the twenty years of the "Golden Age", the average annual sales of Champagne reached 28,733,312 bottles (20,825,314 exported and 7,907,998 sold in France). During the following nine years, the yearly average fell to 21,973,674 bottles (13,447,300 exported and 7,473,774 sold in France).

CHAPTER NINE

The Revolt of the Vignerons

IT WAS ONLY ON DECEMBER 17, 1908, after endless *pourparlers* and pressing demands from both the growers and the shippers of Champagne, that the boundaries or *délimitation* of the *Champagne viticole* were officially defined by decree. None of the vineyards of the Aube *département* were included but for some obscure reason a few vineyards of the Aisne *département* were given the same privilege as those of the Marne of producing wine entitled to the name of Champagne. The wonderful prosperity of the Champagne trade during the Golden Age period had tempted a number of people to become Champagne shippers on their own account. Some of these people were well-to-do *vignerons*, while others were of the type of company promoters always ready; to back any enterprise likely to be profitable; most of them were determined to get rich quickly. They evidently considered that the shortest cut to wealth was to buy wine in the cheapest market, which happened to be Béziers, and to sell it as Champagne, from their Champagne cellars and offices. The *délimitation* decree had been acclaimed by all honest *vignerons* and shippers, that is probably 90 % of the whole, but it really did nothing to stop the misdeeds of the *fraudeurs*, so that the stocks of Champagne bottles in the cellars of

Champagne shippers, which had to be declared to the excise authorities every year, grew appreciably, in spite of the fact that the quantities of Champagne sold had been greater than the quantities produced in the Marne.

Quantity of wine from Marne vineyards

1907	306,457	Hectolitres, or about	29,000,000	botles
1908	127,281	,,	,,	,,	16,000,000
1909	268,200	,,	,,	,,	33,700,000
1910	9,936	,,	,,	,,	1,000,000

Sales of Champagne

1905-1906	35,591,135	bottles
1906-1907	33,171,395	,,
1907-1908	33,734,618	,,
1908-1909	32,705,338	,,
1909-1910	39,294,526	,,
1910-1911	38,584,402	,,

All honest shippers and *vignerons* demanded that it be made obligatory by law to keep the real Champagne wines and the others in separate cellars under the supervision of the excise authorities, and that no wine other than genuine Champagne should be allowed, under very severe penalties, to be sold as Champagne. They did get those *magasins séparés* eventually, in 1912, but only after the Revolt of the Vignerons, in 1911.

The vintage of 1909 was not a small one, but it was a most depressing one; the grapes were picked in cold, wet weather; most of them were of no use at all and some of the *vignerons* of the lower Marne Valley were not even able to find a buyer for their grapes at the panic price of four pence per kilog. There was a great deal of hardship among the small *vignerons* everywhere during the winter of 1909-1910, and the last flicker of hope disappeared when the cold and wet summer of 1910 killed all chances of a decent vintage.

On October 9, 1910, some 500 *vignerons* met at Damery asking that something be done for them; on the 16th, the following Sunday, 10,000 *vignerons* met at Epernay and demanded that the *fraudeurs* should be made to give up importing "foreign" wines into Champagne. On November 8, some 400 *vignerons* rushed the Epernay Goods Yard to smash 60 casks of Midi wines which had just arrived; but they went home after having been promised that the wine would be sent back to Béziers at once. The *vignerons* of Hautvillers, Cumières, Damery, Dizy and Ay formed pickets and kept a watch upon all arrivals by rail or road of wine in casks or bottles. On December 26, 1910, two lorries laden with casks of wine were stopped by a mob of *vignerons*, numbering 500 according to the gendarmes – 1,500, according to the local Press the next day, who gave the time as 5.30 p.m., and the place as near Hautvillers. The mere fact that wine was being moved at night – though not late at night, it was quite dark – was taken as sufficient evidence that it was the wrong sort of wine: in a moment every cask had its head knocked in and the wine was running down the road. On January 17, 1911, a lorry with 2,000 bottles and 300 half-bottles of doubtful Champagne was "captured" by a large concourse of *vignerons* in the yard of a Damery firm, the owner of which was said to sell all the grapes of his Damery vineyard at top prices at the time of the vintage, whilst he sold as Champagne the Midi wine that he bought at the lowest prices. Some of the mob drove the lorry to the Marne and tipped the whole of the wine in the river, whilst the rest sacked and wrecked the man's cellars. By the time the gendarmes arrived, all had gone and there was nothing that they could do.

During the night of 17/18 January, the cellars of a Hautvillers merchant were broken into, and some 100 casks of wine were destroyed.

The local gendarmes were far too few to deal with the growing number of malcontents and their growing audacity, and the authorities called out the army to protect those merchants who were terrified that they might be the next victims of the irate *vignerons*. The one regiment of *Dragons* stationed at Epernay could not cope with the alarming situation, so seven squadrons of *Chasseurs* and two battalions of infantry were sent for and stationed at Ay, Damery, Venteuil, Cumières and Hautvillers, on the right bank of the Marne, overlooking Epernay.

On January 20, the Préfet called a meeting of the *vignerons* and promised to do the best he could to see that no more "foreign" wine be allowed into the region, and the *vignerons* demanded that all merchants sign an undertaking not to import any Midi wine. Most of them agreed.

On February 6, 1911, the law for the *mesures complémentaires* – separate cellars for Champagne and for other wines – was voted by 499 to 41, and on February 10 it was ratified by the Senate. It was published as law on February 11 in the *Journal Officiel*. This was the law which the *vignerons*, and most Champagne shippers also, had been asking for and hoping for. Besides the "separate cellars", it provided for effective means of checking fraudulent practices and much more severe penalties for *fraudeurs*. It was hailed in the whole of the Champagne country as a great victory: flags were out and there was dancing and rejoicing in all the hitherto "occupied" villages: *Dragons*, *Chasseurs* and *Fantassins* were cheered as they went "home".

The Epernay press came out the next day with *Après la crise viticole* leaders. All was now well.

But there had been no rejoicings in the nearby Aube *département*, the chief city of which, Troyes, had been the county town of the old Champagne province. The *vignerons* of the Aube claimed that they were part and parcel of the Champagne country; that for centuries their wines had been bought by the Reims and Epernay merchants as truly Champagne wines; that since the advent of the cheap Midi wines now flooding the Paris market, they had no chance to sell their wines anywhere but in Reims and Epernay. So they demanded that, in fairness to themselves, the *délimitation* decree, which denied to their wines the right to be Champagne, should be done away with.

On April 10 1911, the *députés* of the Aube tabled a *projet de loi* that would cancel all the existing *délimitation* decrees.

When the news reached the Champagne villages on April 11, the *vignerons* were so infuriated that they took the law into their own hands. At 9 o'clock that night, six business houses at Damery were sacked by a wild mob; the same fate befell others at Dizy, at about 10 p.m.; and also at Ay, at 10.30 p.m., before the *Dragons* arrived post haste with drawn swords to disperse the mob.

The next day, April 12, troops kept on pouring in from Reims and Châlons-sur-Marne, to be met with a rain of bottles from windows and rooftops, and hastily erected barricades of upturned lorries, *pupitres*, and broken furniture from looted cellars and private houses. All approaches to Epernay were guarded, and the premises of all the known *fraudeurs* were given priority of protection. But by the evening of the 12th, the half drunken mob cared little for *fraudeurs* or anybody else, and they set fire to the cellars and offices of two of the Ay firms – Ayala and Bissinger – which unfortunately were unguarded simply because all the *vignerons* knew that there had never been any "foreign" wine there.

During the same day, April 12, the *vignerons* of Moussy and others, on the left bank of the Marne, marched in force upon Epernay, and when they reached Pierry, they sacked the cellars of the first firm they came to, before a squadron of *Chasseurs* arrived to disperse them. The Mayor of Pierry came forth to parley with the officer in charge, and whilst they were arguing, many of the rioters dispersed, but not to go home; they managed to reach Epernay through the vineyards, and they had sacked the premises of a known *fraudeur*, on the outskirts of Epernay, before the *Chasseurs* realized that the "enemy" was no longer before them but in their rear.

Not a shot was fired. Not many were hurt. But the damage done was put down at between seven and eight million francs.

From April to September 1911, there were more soldiers in the hillside villages of Champagne than there were *vignerons*! But when the time came to pick the grapes, and very fine grapes they were in 1911, the soldiers had to go to make room for the army of *vendangeurs* who flock to Champagne at vintage time so that the grapes may be gathered quickly whilst the sun shines.

Of course, the law stepped in also, after the *Dragons* and *Chasseurs* had gone, and a hunt began for the guilty. There were, naturally, many anonymous letters and accusations of all kinds, but real evidence was difficult to secure. Curiously enough, many of the rioters were identified by a "documentary" film which the Epernay Director of the Pathé Cinema had taken at the time!

On June 17, 1911, there was a new *décret* to reaffirm the principle of *délimitation*: it also attempted to be fair to everybody and created a *Champagne deuxième zone* for a large number of vineyards outside the Marne. However, it proved unsatisfactory, and a new Law was promised: it took over two years to draft a text likely to be acceptable to all, and the 1914 war broke out before it could be voted. The law did not get a chance to be accepted by *députés* and *sénateurs* until 1927; it became the Law of July 22, 1927, and it is still in force. It has been amended, however, "*complétée*", and otherwise added to since then on more than one occasion, chiefly by the Law of March 30, 1934, the *décrets* of July 30 and September 28, 1935, June 29, 1936, January 13, 1938, and the Law of April 12, 1941, with the usual corrective amendments or *décrets* on September 8, 1941, and May 6, 1942.

The Law of April 12, 1941, was responsible for the creation of the *Comité Interprofessional du Vin de Champagne*, an official organization to which all belong who have anything to do with sparkling Champagne, be they *vignerons*, merchants, brokers, bankers, or the suppliers of corks, bottles or labels. The *Comité* is there to see that all have fair play, a fair wage, a fair wine to sell, and a fair hearing whenever they have a grievance.

The official French excise statistics of stocks of Champagne in merchants' cellars and of sales of Champagne are the most damning evidence that the

Years	Bottles in Merchants' Stocks 1st April	Quantities Exported from April 1st to March 31st	Quantities sold in France from April 1st to March 31st	Total Deliveries for Export and Home Consumption
	Bottles	Bottles	Bottles	Bottles
1907-08	134,917,193	22,212,346	11,522,272	33,734,618
1908-09	131,425,513	19,992,314	12,713,024	32,705,338
1909-10	118,833,866	21,173,580	13,120,946	39,294,526
1910-11	110,277,301	23,066,253	15,517,879	38,584,402
1911-12				
Champagne	92,919,891	20,288,963	9,084,936	29,373,899
Vins Mousseux	6,734,337	3,001,745	3,312,370	6,314,115
1912-13				
Champagne	80,360,357	20,946,534	9,151,110	30,097,644
Vins Mousseux	8,332,414	2,344,060	3,357,085	5,701,150
1913-14				
Champagne	71,373,401	18,410,436	8,134,196	26,544,632
Vins Mousseux	12,567,922	2,752,484	3,961,924	6,714,408
1919-20				
Champagne	71,948,641	13,583,719	9,681,453	23,265,172
Vins Mousseux	4,108,974	1,437,234	2,231,003	3,668,237

vignerons were right when they claimed that much wine sold as Champagne was not really Champagne, but wine from outside the Champagne country, made sparkling in Champagne cellars, wines which had to be entered as *vins mousseux*, after 1911, as distinct from real Champagne.

CHAPTER TEN

The War and Post-war Years

THE FIRST WORLD WAR WAS A CATASTROPHE of such unprecedented magnitude that it affected everybody in France; the people of Champagne, their vineyards and their wine were among the worst sufferers.

During the last week of August 1914, the whole of the Champagne country was overrun by the Germans hurrying on to Paris. The battle of the Marne halted them just in time; they were pushed back, beyond Reims, during the two first weeks of September, but not very far beyond Reims. The French Army and the British Expeditionary Force were by then fatigued and out of munitions; they could do no more.

The damage done to the vineyards of Champagne during those three historic weeks was trifling, and, soon after, when the time came to gather in the 1914 vintage, some beautiful grapes were picked in beautiful weather, but too few were there to pick or to buy them. It was obviously hazardous for shippers to buy grapes for new wine when the Germans were entrenched uncomfortably near at La Pompelle, but the *vignerons* had no capital, nor anything like an adequate supply of the indispensable casks; somebody had to buy their grapes

Plate 7 CRAYÈRES. Ancient chalk pits and modern galleries connecting them in which millions of bottles of Champagne grow better every day as they await their call.

and send in casks for the new wine. There was no railway, no telegraph and no telephone for civilian use so near the front line, hence there was much anxiety among the *vignerons*: they could not get in touch with the shippers of Reims and Epernay who usually bought their grapes and provided the casks for the new wine.

It was, indeed, fortunate that the Mayor of Epernay at the time was a man of exceptional courage and vision. His name, Maurice Pol Roger, will long be remembered gratefully by the inhabitants of Epernay, and the Champagne *vignerons*. During the occupation of Epernay by the Germans, from the 4th to the 11th September, Maurice Pol Roger dealt with their many requests single-handed – all civil servants and bank staffs had fled to Paris with all public and other funds! – with great courage and success. Soon after, as the time for the vintage was at hand, it was he who organized a service of riders who carried instructions and funds to the *vignerons*, enabling them to get casks and to pay their way for the time being, so that those beautiful grapes could be picked in beautiful weather and good wine be made. There were 200,000 hectolitres of Champagne made in 1914, about half the quantity which had been predicted at the beginning of August. The vintage started on September 21 and lasted until October 11, being longer than usual owing to the shortage of pickers.

The Germans had also been out of munitions in September, but not for long, as the *vignerons* of the Montagne de Reims, who lived in the villages that face Reims and the *route nationale* from Reims to Châlons-sur-Marne, learnt only too soon. Their vineyards, chiefly those of Mailly, Ludes, Verzenay, Sillery, Verzy, Villers-Marmery and Trépail, suffered a great deal more than the other Champagne vineyards from occasional shell-fire, communication trenches, barbed wire and military occupation during four consecutive years. Much worse damage, however, was done by the vine louse, the accursed *Phylloxera vastatrix*, the progress of which could not be checked during that long time Of their 4,685 acres of vines in production in 1914, there were but 2,602 acres left in 1918, which meant that 44.4 % of the vineyards of those villages would have to be cleared, cleaned, rested and then replanted with Pinot grapes grafted on American pest-resisting stock.

Incidentally, unlike the *Phylloxera vastatrix* which was unscared by gunfire, the herds of wild boar which provided the main hunting sport in Champagne completely disappeared from the forests of the Montagne de Reims: nobody ever saw them go, and not one was seen during five years. Then they all returned, but never told where they had spent the war years!

The other vineyards of the Montagne de Reims, those facing East and South, like Bouzy, Ambonnay, Tours-sur-Marne, Avenay, Mareuil-sur-Ay, Ay-Champagne, Dizy, Champillon, Hautvillers and Cumières, were free from barbed wire and communication trenches, but they suffered from the lack of fertilizers and of those chemicals so necessary to check the inroads of insect pests and various diseases of the vines: their pre-war 5,160 acres of vineyards had been reduced to 3,436 acres at the time of the 1918 vintage, a loss of 15.7 %.

The other vineyards of the Marne suffered more or less during the war years, rather less, however, than those of the Montagne de Reims, and, in round figures, there were 16,000 acres of vines in production in 1918, instead of 25,000 acres in 1914. What made matters worse, however, was the fact that only a little more than half the vines still in production in 1918 were Pinots grafted on American stock and likely to stand up to the phylloxera for a few more years to come, whereas there were still 7,500 acres of old French vines on their own roots: these were doomed to death at no distant date with the *phylloxera* in full cry through the land. This meant that about 60 % of the whole of the Marne vineyards would have to be replanted at once and some 30 % more would have to be dug up and replaced soon after. A grim outlook!

As regards the wine, there was a great deal of very fair wine made during the war years, chiefly in 1915 and 1917, but 1914 and 1918 were not at all bad vintages, and even in 1916, the worst of the war vintages, some decent wine was made. More and better wine was produced during the three immediate post-war vintages, chiefly in 1921, but unfortunately the standard of quality of the Champagne made during the war and postwar years was not, on the whole, equal to the pre-war standard. There were some outstanding *cuvées* sold by a few of the first rank shippers, but they were the exception and not the rule.

What had happened?

The *délimitation* had given the exclusive right to the name "Champagne" to the wines of a limited number of villages within the borders of the Marne *département*: many of those villages, not to say all of them, did not live by wine

alone: they had orchards and grasslands as well as vineyards, and in a number
of them there was green grass near the riverside full of daisies and buttercups.
Surely grapes could grow there instead and pay a better dividend? Which is
why, soon after the war, when losses had to be made good as soon as possible,
vines were planted in alluvial soil, near the Marne; they brought forth an
abundance of grapes, a much greater quantity of bunches per vine than the
same vine ever produced in the nearby hillside vineyards. More grapes certainly,
but not nearly the same quality of wine. Yet who could challenge the right
of such wine to the name of "Champagne"? It was made from grapes grown
in the very heart of the Marne, in places bearing the most illustrious names in
the vinous annals of Champagne.

The law had to step in, and now it is illegal to sell as "Champagne" any
sparkling wine made from grapes grown within the *région délimitée de la
Champagne viticole*, if and when the yield of the native grapes has been superior
to 50 hectolitres per hectare, that is about 500 gallons per acre, a quantity much
below that of the yield of vines grown in "rich" land – for rich land is the
mother of "poor" wine.

Another cause of the lower standard of quality of much Champagne made
during the war and post-war years was the greater use of *tailles*, the name given
to second and third pressings of Champagne grapes. According to tradition,
the normal load of the press in Champagne is 4,000 kilogs, of grapes, which
yield 20 hectolitres (440 gallons) of the best grape-juice. Then comes a second
pressing, which yields a further 3 hectolitres of a wine less excellent than the
first; the next pressing, however, which is also expected to yield another 3
hectolitres of wine, is distinctly inferior; as to the fourth pressing, which gets
every trace of moisture out of what is left of the grapeskins, it is called *rebèche*
and is no good at all by itself.

Before the war, that is to say up to the spring of 1914, a great deal of all the
tailles – second and third pressings – of Champagne were bought by the Germans for their national sparkling wine called Sekt, not necessarily a German
wine, but a wine made in Germany, which the Germans law allows to be made
from any suitable wine. They could not have bought a cheaper or more suitable
wine anywhere else.

After 1918, the Germans had no currency, even if they had had the wish, to buy any wine in Champagne. Somebody had to drink the *tailles*, which were, after all, perfectly genuine Champagne wines, and so they went into blends of the less expensive, well sugared, brands of Champagne, the kind which, more often than not, are served at wedding receptions and official functions, or sold in Paris night-clubs.

Once more, however, the law intervened, making it illegal to sell as "Champagne" any wine made from grapes grown within the *région délimitée* when the quantity of wine made from such grapes had been more than one hectolitre per 150 kilogs. of grapes, a figure which allows the whole of the second pressing and a third of the third pressing to be blended with the first, but none of the wine of the last pressing. Since most Champagne shippers offer for sale a range of different brands, some sweeter than others, some dearer than others, they are at liberty to use the cheaper *tailles* as they think best.

Great as was the damage suffered by the Champagne vineyards during the years of the First World War, it was eventually made good by hard work and hard cash. Not so, unfortunately, the loss of some two thirds of Champagne export markets. There were no more Grand Dukes in Russia nor Magyars in Hungary; no more gay social life in Vienna and Warsaw; the blight of Prohibition had sealed the United States market and was affecting materially the Scandinavian countries. All this meant that most of the people, outside France and England, who had known and loved Champagne before the war, could no longer afford it, and those who could afford it had the means but had lost the chance to buy it. Under such conditions, the English market was of paramount importance to the people of Champagne.

When the First World War came to an end, in November 1918, the traditional distribution of Champagne in the British Isles, and many parts of the world within what was known at the time as the British Empire, was still what it had been before the outbreak of the war, when Champagne was sold by the shippers and their agents to wholesalers, market houses, retailers, who were either private wine-merchants or grocers, and stores; also the more important hotels, restaurants, railway and shipping companies, and other caterers. The agents of the shippers sold non-vintage Champagne all the year and every year in 30 dozen lots; they also sold every two or three years' vintage *cuvées en bloc*, that is, at one and the same time, the whole of the quantity of any vintage *cuvée*

which their principals at Reims, Epernay or Ay had to sell. In the case of all the popular brands of Champagne, when the agents announced that such or such a vintage would be available at such or such a price, a time limit used to be given beyond which no more orders for the wine would be considered. That was the date when all orders received would be added up by the agents, who would then proceed to the business of alloting to each of the would-be buyers whatever proportion of their original order could be spared, so that the total figure for the sales did not exceed the total figure for the *cuvée* which the shippers had given to their agents to sell. Within a few days of the "allotment" of the vintage *cuvée* of a popular brand, the market price would be from 10 to 12 shillings up, and, within a year or so, the "stock" might well be 20s. or 30s. up per dozen bottles, the price of the vintage appreciating from year to year according to the demand. The supply, of course, did not follow the demand; whatever quantity had originally been alloted could be relied upon to be the final figure.

The war changed all that. To begin with, the initial cost of Champagne was much higher immediately after the war when the duty rose from 7s.6d. per dozen bottles to 31s. This new rate of duty, comparatively high as it was then, was more acceptable to the wine trade than the *ad valorem* duty on Champagne which followed; it was introduced by the greatest Englishman of the age, but by no means the best Chancellor of the Exchequer: with typical Churchillian bulldog tenacity, he refused to listen to the Customs and Excise authorities; he claimed that it was not fair to make the rich and the poor pay the same tax – that is, on the top price fashionable brands of Champagne, and the cheapest sparkling wine bearing a fancy label and costing about half the price of the others. Fair or not, the *ad valorem* duty did not work: on every shipment of Champagne there was a different rate of duty, and the prices at which some shippers invoiced their wines became quite surprisingly low.

In spite of higher duties and also higher prices demanded by the shippers, the London agents of all the better known shippers had no difficulty in selling the vintage wines which their principals had to offer as soon as the war was over, and when means of transport became available. Stocks of Champagne in merchants' cellars and in private houses were at the lowest ebb after four and a half years when so little Champagne had come from France. The taste for Champagne had not been lost: on the contrary, it was a case of "absence makes the heart grow fonder". What had been lost, however, was the investment value of vintage Champagne. Pre-war vintages – 1899, 1900, 1904, 1906 – did not cost more on the whole than 80 shillings per dozen, duty paid, *en primeur*, and all the more popular brands fetched 160 shillings per dozen within a remarkable short time. The war and post-war vintages – 1915, 1917, 1919 – cost about 150 shillings per dozen, *en primeur*, and they never had a chance of reaching 200 shillings per dozen, however long one might have waited.

What made matters ever so much worse in the 'twenties, was the erratic behaviour of the French franc. Up to 1914, the rate of exchange of the franc had been 25.22½ francs to the pound sterling, but by March 1919 it had eased a little to 25.97 francs: by December of the same year, it had slipped to 41 francs to the pound, and twelve months later to 60 francs, settling down at 124.20 from March 1927 for a while, with some ups and downs from time to time. An erratic rate of exchange is bound to introduce an element of gambling in all commercial transactions, but what made it worse than ever in the Champagne trade was the fact that the wine-merchant who had bought and paid for his stock of Champagne at a time when he could not get more than 60 francs for £1, could not compete with the person who had bought the same wine, or at any rate a wine that bore the same brand, when the pound was worth 124 francs.

It was not merely difficult to do business under such conditions; it was impossible for merchants and the old "market houses" to hold stocks, as had been the tradition in the wine trade in England for generations. The situation had a distinctly demoralising effect all round. One of the more popular shippers of Champagne, anxious as all were to protect their English customers from unfair competition, decided to ship to the British Isles none but odd-year vintages – 1915, 1917, 1919, 1921, 1923 – and elsewhere none but even-year vintages – 1914, 1916, 1918, 1920. It certainly looked as if he did not attach much, if any, value to the idea that a vintage Champagne is the wine of the particular year of which it bears the date, but, as it happened, there were good enough wines made in practically all years from 1913 to 1923, wines that could be shipped as vintage wines.

In France, the impact of the erratic behaviour of the franc was quite different. Trading conditions were also entirely different, most of the important Champagne shippers having their offices and trade counters in Paris and other important cities, as well as commercial travellers selling their wine directly to restaurants, hotels, grocers, wine-merchants, and private customers, according to a price stucture that gave the caterer and the retailer a chance to sell at a profit to the public the same wine which the public could buy from the shippers. When the French franc came unpegged, in 1919, and went from bad to worse during the 'twenties, it shattered the age-long belief of the average Frenchman and Frenchwoman in the virtue of saving, of stuffing the *bas de laine* with money saved *sou* by *sou*. Money was no longer worth saving: only goods had any real value; and having "a good time" appeared to be more sensible than thrift. And the official statistics are there to show that as and when the franc depreciated, up and up went the consumption of Champagne in France. There must have been more and more French people at the time who realized that they knew how to drink Champagne on the other side of the Channel, and they, also, could and did enjoy Champange *à l'anglaise*, not just one little *flûte* of Champagne, mostly gas, but in a proper wine glass, to drink, not to sip. It is quite certain, and not in the least surprising, that the consumption of Champagne in France has never ceased to grow, so that now twice as much Champagne is drunk in France as is exported to all the markets of the world; this is the reverse of the position that had existed up to 1921.

CHAPTER ELEVEN

The Difficult Years

VAUVENARGUES, WHO HAD IN HIS CHEQUERED career a greater share of troubles than most of us, once wrote that the world in which we live was made for intelligent people, since it is full of difficulties. Whether the people of Champagne were sufficiently intelligent to appreciate that all was as it should be, we cannot tell, but they certainly had a most generous helping of difficulties to cope with, not only during the First World War, but ever since those fateful years. Nature appears to have done her best to help the Champenois and to make good, during the 'twenties, their appalling war losses: four fine vintages in one decade is an uncommon thing in Champagne, and the 1920, 1921, 1928 and 1929 vintages all brought forth a great deal of very good wines. Two other vintages of the same decade, 1923 and 1926, were also responsible for a good quantity of very fair wines, and as to the rest of the vintages of the 'twenties, though they were not as good as these, they were by no means bad.

The tragedy was that economic conditions throughout the world had been so disastrously affected by the First World War, that the great majority of the world's population had no money to spare for anything over and above the more immediate necessaries of existence; the joy that is Champagne was beyond their reach.

Whilst stocks were piling up in their cellars, the Champagne shippers were also worried by the nightmare of Prohibition which was being actively advocated by fanatical crusaders. It was then that the *Ligue des Adversaires des Prohibitions* was formed by liberty-loving and worried wine producers, with Champagne shippers in the vanguard and Bertrand de Mun, Chairman of Veuve Clicquot, as their leader.

There was much Champagne sold at home and abroad during the 'twenties, but it took a great deal of hard work and hard cash to sell. The growers were by no means happy: they had to sell their grapes at prices which were too low at a time when the cost of living was constantly rising, and the shippers were no better off; they had to reduce their prices in order to reduce their stocks, in spite of the fact that their overheads had never been so high.

The first three Champagne vintages of the 'thirties were very disappointing: there was but little wine made and none of it was any good. This was a catastrophe for the *vignerons*, most of whom got deeper and deeper in debt, but it was not so disastrous for the shippers, more particularly those who did not own any or many vineyards: they had large stocks of 1928 and 1929 wines that would soon be ready for sale. For most of them, the best export market was the United Kingdom and the then British Empire, Australia, South Africa, Canada, Malaya, the Far East - Shanghai and Hong Kong – and so on, at a time when the United States were still in the grip of Prohibition.

Up to October 31, 1931, every 20 shillings due to Champagne shippers meant 620 francs to pay for the grapes at the next vintage, and to meet all their many commitments. But when on that fatal day the Bank of England gave up the gold standard, every 20 shillings due to the Champagne shippers meant only 420 francs. It was indeed a serious blow, and the only logical thing that the Champagne shippers could do was to raise their prices. Unfortunately it was in practice the last thing they could do. The devaluation of the pound had been such a bitter blow to British morale that all luxuries were taboo, and a national wave of austerity set in which affected everybody, but more particularly the richer people. At the Embassy Club in London, for instance, where Champagne had flowed nightly for so long, bottled beer replaced Champagne in the

Champagne coolers, and it was considered bad taste to order any Champagne anywhere. How could the Champagne shippers increase the price of their brands under such conditions? It would not have increased the demand: it would probably have killed it outright.

It is all very well to say that we can never have too much good wine, but there are exceptions to all rules and there can be too much good wine in bad times, as the 'thirties certainly were. One easily realises how unwelcome the fine vintage of 1934 was, and still more so the more abundant vintage of 1935, if one compares the official statistics of quantities of Champagne in shippers' cellars in 1919 and 1934, on the one hand, and the quantities of Champagne exported in those same years:

	No. of bottles in Champagne cellars	No. of bottles exported
1919	71,948,641	13,583,719
1934	146,582,250	4,559,030

Two good vintages could not have come at worse time, a time of world economic crisis, when the Champagne trade, a luxury trade, was already sorely hit by the slump. A great deal of the 1935 Champagne wines never sparkled: they were sold as still table wines at prices which did not repay the *vignerons* for their costly fight against the many enemies of the grape, and the constant care which must be given to their vines.

There was at the time a fair quantity of still wines of Champagne sold in France, and a small quantity sold abroad, but the lesson which the 1934 vintage taught the vignerons was that they must no longer be so entirely dependent upon the shippers for the sale of their grapes, or of the new wine made therefrom. Many of them decided that in future they must make their own wine, still or sparkling, but sparkling for choice. This, however, was not very easy. To make sparkling wine from one's own grapes means in the first instance that somebody must come forward and offer a substantial sum of money at a reasonable rate of interest. This is the first and also the easiest hurdle for the *vigneron* to negotiate. What is much more difficult is to secure suitable premises, and the necessary equipment for keeping, handling and dealing with the grapes, and the wine made from them, during the long and intricate process that is responsible for changing sweet, turbid grape-juice into a clear, lively, sparkling wine. Obviously this was beyond the capacities of all but a very few of the more important *vignerons*, and so the others did what has been done in other branches of agriculture: they decided to put up their money and their grapes together and to form cooperative associations that were to own and to operate suitable premises, fully equipped with all modern machinery, to handle large quantities of grapes sent in at the time of the vintage by a large number of *vignerons*, mostly small and very small men unable to deal with their crop themselves. Eventually each one of those *vignerons* would be entitled to his proper share of the profit arising from the sale of the communal wine, after the deduction of overheads and other expenses.

Black as the clouds were over the Champagne skies in 1934, there came a welcome silver lining with the Repeal, in 1933, of the Volstead Act, the American Prohibition Law. Champagne shippers crossed the Atlantic in droves to appoint agents and find out for themselves what were the chances of creating or reviving a worthwhile demand for their brands in the United States. What was badly wanted at the time was not commercial travellers hawking their wares, but missionaries who might persuade the young people of America that Champagne was the fairway, as opposed to the out-of-bounds of hard liquor and soft drinks.

Repeal certainly brought a very welcome ray of new hope to both the *vignerons* and shippers of Champagne, and the first export figures that followed were quite encouraging. They rose from 7,854,962 bottles in 1935-6, to 11,735,287 bottles in 1936-7, and to 11,957,426 bottles in 1937-8.

Then, as the vintage of 1939 was about to be harvested, came the Second World War, which for the people of Champagne meant four years of total occupation, massive requisitions, shortages of almost everything from fertilizers for the vines to bottles and corks for the wine; and, of course, it also meant the loss of all export markets other than Germany!

In the United Kingdom, very little wine could be imported during the first three years of the war, and not a great deal during the following three years. In March 1940, however, there were 12.5 million gallons of Champagne in the country's bonded stocks of wine, and as there were but 2.2 million gallons left by March 1945, it had been well worthwhile for various Chancellors of the Exchequer to raise the duty on wine, beginning with September 28, 1939, and rising steadily until 1947.[a]

Although wine had become subject to import licences in June 1940, it was freely admitted under Open General Licence until March 1941, from which date licences for ordinary trade importations of wine were no longer granted. In 1945, following on negotiations between the Treasury, the Ministry of Food, the French exporters and the Wine and Spirit Association, import licences were made available by the Ministry of Food and the Board of Trade in respect of Champagne and other French wines and spirits, the conditions of sale being laid down at the time as follows: –

The Ministry of Food insist, as one of the conditions of the present concession, that importers and all other firms dealing in the wines and spirits must take every precaution to see that the maximum re-selling prices, as fixed by agreement between the Wine and Spirit Association and the Ministry of Food, are not exceeded, and that

the wines and spirits do not find their way into the 'Black Market' or other undesirable hands.

Datum years. 1935, 1936, 1937, 1938, 1939.

Quantities. The amount of approximately 175,000 cases between now and the end of the year.

Qualities. There will be four types as follows:-

No. 1. Grandes Marques Vintage at a price to the importer of 130s. per case f.o.b. Channel Port.

No. 2. Grandes Marques Non-vintage at a price to the importer of 115s. per case f.o.b. Channel Port.

No. 3. Buyers Own Brands Vintage at a price to the importer of 115s. per case f.o.b. Channel Port.

No. 4. Buyers Own Brands Non-vintage at a price to the importer 100s. per case f.o.b. Channel Port.

Prices. The Retail prices per bottle have been agreed with the Ministry of Food, and the intermediate trade prices have been determined in agreement with the trade associations concerned. These prices must not be exceeded.

	No. 1	No. 2	No. 3	No. 4
Cost to the wholesaler, delivered into customer's bond, per case	167s.	149s.	142s.	124s. 6d.
Cost to the wholesaler, duty paid and delivered, per case.	245s.	227s.	220s.	202s. 6d.
Cost to retailer	279s.	255s.	252s.	234s.
Cost to public per bottle.	28s.	25s.	25s.	23s.
Cost to public per half-bottle	14s.	13s.	13s.	12s.
Half-bottles – 12s. extra per case of 24 half bottles.				
Restaurant price per bottle	59s.	53s. 6d.	53s. 6d.	50s.
Restaurant price per half-bottle	30s.	27s. 9d.	27s. 9d.	26s.

According to the Customs and Excise figures relating to the "home consumption" (duty payments) of Champagne during the war and immediate post-war years, the quantities were as follows:-

1938-39	482,382 *gallons*
1939-40	344,810
1940-41	207,543
1941-42	67,189
1942-43	26,520
1943-44	11,821
1944-45	8,691
1945-46	86,756
1946-47	297,439
1947-48	326,361
1948-49	345,862
1949-50	439,055

NOTES

^a Duties on Champagne imported into the United Kingdom (per gallon)

1938-39	16s. 6d.
1939-40	18s. 6d.
1940-41	20s. 6d.
1941-43	32s. 9d.
1943-44	39s. od.
Nov. 1947	44s. od.
April 1948	37s. 6d.
April 1960	27s. 6d.
April 1961	30s. od.

Plate 8 REMUAGE. The peculiar perforated double boards, known as *pupitres*, used to get the sediment in the wine to slide down and to collect it upon the inside face of the cork, ready for the *dégorgeur* to get rid of it.

CHAPTER TWELVE

Champagne Today

WHEN CHAMPAGNE SPARKLED for the first time, it sparkled at the Court of the Merrie Monarch, in England, in the 'sixties of the seventeenth century, and during the next two hundred years or so, Champagne was the favourite and the privilege of the rich and the great in many lands. Champagne was the wine they drank at Versailles and the Petit Trianon before the French Revolution, and at the Tuileries in Paris, at the heyday of Napeoleon III's reign: Champagne was the wine of the aristocrats of finance and shipping in Boston, New York and Philadelphia, when Lincoln was President of the United States; and it was also the wine of the less aristocratic gold diggers of California in the 1840s. Champagne was the wine of Frederick the Great of Prussia, the patron of the arts and the friend of Voltaire; and Champagne sparkled in crystal glasses on the tables of the great ducal Houses of England, noted for their hospitality, as well as at Westminster and at the board of the more "common", but not less generous, generations that grew up after the Industrial Revolution.

Champagne was the wine of Tsars, of Grand Dukes and other proud aristocrats of Imperial Russia and Austria-Hungary from the eighteenth century to the First World War. All have now passed away. Not so Champagne! Its prestige was never higher than it is today: its message of goodwill and gaiety now cheers a far greater number of people than ever before.

Champagne still is, and must ever be, an expensive wine, but there are now many more people than before with a taste for what is best, and a chance to get it. They must have Champagne.

The taste for Champagne is not new: it is three hundred years old. What is new, or comparatively new, is the popular liking, one might call it the craze, for sparkling wines, any wine that has plenty of gas in it. Champagne has long ceased to be the only wine with bubbles in it. There are plenty of other wines just as sparkling, which does not mean just as good, and they mostly cost much less than Champagne, which is why sparkling wines are now enjoyed by all but the really poor, in the U.S.S.R. as well as anywhere else.

Champagne is costly because the grapes from which it is made are costly, more costly since the last war than they ever were before; because it takes a long time and many skilled, highly paid people to make it to perfection; because it has to be given time to "mellow" in bottle, and rates of interest on capital bottled and locked up for five, six or more years[a] are high. So, in the end, Champagne costs more, but it is also *worth* more.

There is no reason, however, why people who like sparkling wine and cannot afford the price of Champagne should not be given the chance to enjoy wines within their means, wines with as much gas as any Champagne has. Gas is still cheap.

The Russians claim that their scientists have perfected a method for speeding up the making of "Champagne". This seems to amount to some sort of pepping up of the secondary fermentation in *cuve close*, or tanks, by the addition of yeast, after which the wine is bottled and given – or sold – right away. Let them!

In Germany, there are some very good sparkling wines made from grapes grown in Germany and sold under the name of their native vineyards, but there are also far greater quantities of sparkling wines made from any wine which the makers choose to import from any source; such wines must be sold as Sekt, or under any fancy name other than a geographical name. In 1960, there were 71 million bottles of such wines sold, and 49 million bottles of Champagne, a record figure for Champagne. There is no reason why more and cheaper Sekt may not be made in the years to come: it is not handicapped, as Champagne is, by any geographical limitations.

There are likewise considerable quantities of sparkling wines made in Spain, Portugal and Italy, and also in the United States of America; fairly large quantities are also made in Australia, South Africa, the Argentine, Chile, indeed in practically all wine-producing countries.

But the supremacy of Champagne remains unquestioned. It would be foolish, of course, to claim that all Champagne is good and that it must invariably be better than any other sparkling wine. It is not so. But the best Champagne is better than the best of all sparkling wines. If it were not so, the demand for Champagne would not be greater today than it has ever been, in spite of the challenge of so many other sparkling wines available in all parts of the world at lower prices than Champagne. Official statistics are there as evidence of the world-wide popularity of Champagne.

Champagne has never before had so wide and varied a public. The best of all Champagne customers are the British, when they are at home, of course, and in every part of the globe where they travel, settle and have clubs. More Champagne is imported into the United Kingdom every year than into any other country. What is even more remarkable is that a very large proportion of all the best vintage *cuvées* of Champagne come to England, dearer though they are than other Champagne. There is also nowadays in England a greater cross-section of the population than anywhere else who appreciate the characteristics of Champagne sufficiently to demand it, if not habitually, occasionally, according to their means.

The United States do not buy quite as much Champagne as Great Britain, although their population and wealth are so very much greater. By far the greatest proportion of Americans who like sparkling wines are perfectly happy with any of the many American brands from New York State, New Jersey, Ohio or California. Some of them know that there is such a place as Champagne somewhere in France and that the "original" Champagne is still made there. There is, however, in the United States, as in other countries, a number of highly educated, much travelled, wealthy and cultured men and women of taste who know the difference between good, better and best, and who demand the best: they are responsible for the consumption of some three million bottles of the more popular brands of Champagne every year.

The third largest buyer of Champagne is Belgium, not to mention the Belgians of the former Belgian Congo who, up to 1960, bought much Champagne. Most of the Champagne bought by the Belgians, however, is of the non-vintage type – quite good wine, though younger, sweeter and cheaper than vintage Champagne.

Fourth place among Champagne's "million-bottles-a-year" customers has now been taken by Italy, the rise in the demand for Champagne apparently being due to the rise of the film industry in that country.

Looking through the figures for the sales of Champagne to the world during the past few years, one notices that there is an appreciable demand for Champagne wherever there happens to be oil – in places as widely apart as the Persian Gulf and Venezuela. Obviously where there is oil there is money, and where there is money, Champagne gets its chance.

One of the most spectacular changes to take place in the Champagne trade since the First World War has been the rapid rise in the volume of sales of Champagne by the *vignerons* direct to the public, mostly through their cooperative societies. Some ninety-nine per cent of the Champagne they sell is non-vintage wine, young and sweet, wine suited to the taste and pockets of the

Sales of Champagne from 1951 to 1960 by Shippers and Vignerons

	SHIPPERS	VIGNERONS	TOTAL
1951	32,269,127	2,952,520	35,221,647
1952	27,393,841	3,134,720	30,528,561
1953	27,063,407	3,303,492	30,366,899
1954	29,146,383	3,831,397	32,977,780
1955	32,954,646	4,752,180	37,706,826
1956	38,481,668	5,822,529	44,304,197
1957	40,570,615	7,851,504	48,422,119
1958	33,177,536	7,524,755	40,702,291
1959	34,341,152	7,928,921	42,270,073
1960	39,006,198	10,259,303	49,265,501

people of France and Belgium. The shippers, with larger reserves of old wines and also with long standing connections in the various markets of the world, though they sell a great deal of Champagne in France, are responsible for practically the whole of the Champagne which is exported to foreign countries. The wines they sell are mostly older, better and dearer vintage wines.

The wines sold by shippers and *vignerons* are by no means the same, although they are all made within the legal limits of the *délimitation* and are all equally entitled to the name of Champagne. They differ basically on account of the difficulty for the *vignerons* of making Champagne in the traditional manner which gave Dom Pérignon's wines their superiority over all others: that is, the happy blending of wines made from grapes grown in different Champagne vineyards. In many cases, this is impossible for them. Most *vignerons* have no choice but to sell the Champagne made from the grapes of their own vineyards. This is, of course, what the Marquis de Sillery, and others did three hundred years ago, before Dom Pérignon had come to Hautvillers.

Champagne from the grapes of one Champagne village can indeed be very good, but Champagne made from a blend of black and white Pinots, some from the Montagne de Reims vineyards, some from the Valley of the Marne, and some from the Côte des Blancs, is a much better wine, more balanced, more complete and also more lasting, not merely keeping alive for a greater number of years, but gaining power as well as charm with age. The "single" Champagne of most *vignerons* is not made to last: it is made to be drunk as soon as possible, when its freshness and lower cost are very real assets, appealing particularly to those wine-merchants who make a speciality of selling, under some fancy name or brand, invented and registered by them, a cheaper Champagne than that which bears the famous name of one of the *Grandes Marques*.

The Champagne made and sold by *vignerons* varies greatly in quality and style according to the soil, sub-soil, elevation and aspect of their different vineyards; also according to the professional skill and working facilities of different *vignerons* or of the Cooperative handling their wines. The same may be said to apply to a certain extent to the wines sold by the shippers, large and small, old-established or newcomers alike. All shippers have their own technique and standards, and most of them have vineyards in all parts of the *Champagne viticole*, although not in the same proportion everywhere.

At the time of the 1934 and 1935 vintages, when shippers and *vignerons* were so grievously short of money, whilst they had more wine than they could sell, a Committee was formed (in 1935) which was known as *Commission Spéciale de Champagne*, with Comte Robert de Voguë representing the shippers, and Maurice Doyard representing the *vignerons*, both men who richly deserve the gratitude of the people of Champagne. Little did they know at the time that this *Commission spéciale* would have to deal, a few years later, with the *Bureau de la Viticulture*, set up in Reims by the Germans to run in their own way, as they thought, the Champagne trade. The *Commission* was superseded by an *Arrêté* of November 11th 1940, or rather converted into a *Bureau National de répartition du Vin de Champagne*, with Headquarters at the Préfecture of Châlons-sur-Marne; but this *Bureau* had a short lease of life: it was replaced by a new official body, on April 12 1941, known as the *Comité Interprofessionnel du Vin de Champagne*, or C.I.V.C. for short, and it has been responsible for the "good conduct" of *vignerons* and shippers alike from that day to this.

The C.I.V.C. has brought into the production and distribution of Champagne a measure of discipline which may be more in the German than in the French tradition, but it has proved to be of real value and benefit to the great majority of *vignerons* and shippers. They all have to do what they are told, and this cannot be at all times to their liking, but they all recognize that the C.I.V.C. is constantly and impartially doing its best for the common good.

The margin of profit which the C.I.V.C. allows cannot be called excessive, and there are no hopes today of fabulous fortunes to be made by growing grapes in Champagne or selling Champagne, even should the sun come out again in all its glory as it did in 1893 and 1900. On the other hand, there is no fear today of any revolt of the *vignerons* as happened in 1911, and there are better conditions of living throughout the vinelands of Champagne.

For many years, not to say for many centuries, the price paid at the time of the vintage for either the grapes or the newly made wine fluctuated with the two important factors of quantity and quality. Thus in 1952, when a moderate quantity of wine (7,354,000 gallons) of very fine quality was made, the price of the *Hors Classe Catégorie* grapes was 155 francs per kilog., roughly equivalent to 40 shillings ($5.60) per gallon of wine. In 1953, when rather less (7,000,000 gallons) of very good quality wine was made, the price of the grapes rose to

160 francs per kilog., or about 42 shillings ($5.88) per gallon of new wine. In 1954, there was a greater quantity (8,344,000 gallons) of wine made, but it was of quite poor quality, in spite of which the *Hors Classe Catégorie* grapes were paid for at the rate of 138 francs per kilog., or about 34 shillings ($4.76) per gallon of new wine. In 1955, when there were better and more grapes (10,351,000 gallons), the *Hors Classe Catégorie* grapes were paid for at the rate of 141 francs per kilog., or about 36 shillings ($5.04) per gallon. In 1960 there was double the quantity of grapes vintaged in Champagne than were harvested in 1959: unfortunately they were not nearly such fine grapes. Normally, when the quantity is up and the quality down, one would expect the grapes to cost less, but in 1960 the vignerons were paid a higher price for their grapes than in 1959 – 3 N.F. per kilog. or about 9s. per lb ($1.40). Why? Because the price of Champagne had gone up and the prices of the grapes – good or bad – had to keep in step with the price of the wine. So, in 1961, when the quantity of grapes vintaged was much smaller than in 1960, and their quality was very much better, as the selling price of Champagne had remained the same, the price of the 1961 grapes was the same as in 1960, 3 N.F. per kilog. or about 9s. ($1.40) per lb.

The C.I.V.C. has done much for the Champagne trade, but it cannot be held responsible for one of the more spectacular changes in the Champagne-making technique as adopted by all the most important shippers. For centuries past, young wine and old oak have lived together quite happily, but of course there never was any question of marriage. The newly born wine left the oak fermenting vat for oak hogsheads, and finally found itself in great oak *foudres* before being shut up in glass bottles. The wine was young and the oak was old, but by no means dead, and it could give to the wine a touch of tannin, or something of the kind, besides allowing a little oxygen to seep through the staves. Of course, one stave with a spot of mould could be fatal to the wine, and there was also the danger of some microscopic bug burrowing itself into the oak and turning up in the wine. These were risks which are inevitable wherever there is life. There are no risks of this kind now that the newly made wine no longer comes into contact with the oak of casks: from the moment it leaves the *pressoir* until it is bottled six, seven, or eight months later, its short life is spent in glass-lined steel containers, in which it runs no risk of conta-

mination whatever: it is all the time under perfect control and demands the attention of a very few, instead of a great many, men.

This is the most obvious change, but the most important must surely be the present scientific evolution in the making of Champagne. *Chefs de cave* are no longer what they used to be. The first whom I knew, some 65 years ago, was called Victor Lambert: he was a self-educated *paysan champenois* with a heart of gold, which is not so uncommon, whatever pessimists may say; his sense of smell and of taste were quite exceptional among humans. His method of tasting was not at all scientific. He put a teaspoonful of sugar in a dozen glasses, which he then filled with new wine from a dozen different vineyards. He would then ask me to tell him what I thought of each wine. "*Mais*, Monsieur Lambert," I protested, "they are all the same to me, I can only smell the sugar." "Of course you can smell the sugar, *mon p'tit*," old Victor Lambert would explain patiently, "you can smell the sugar and you can also see it in each glass, but try again and you will find that all those wines are slightly different: the sugar is there as a uniform background against which slight differences will stand out." Certainly a most unscientific method of making a *cuvée*, in spite of which Victor Lambert had been responsible for the 1874, 1889 and 1892 – his last – *cuvées* among others which made the reputation and the fortune of his firm.

His successor of today is a scientist with many diplomas and an impressive list of initials after his name. He has a laboratory full of uncanny instruments that tell him all there is to know about the wines under his control, and the wines he makes are very good. But I would dearly love to believe that he may one day make as fine wines as old Victor did.

NOTES

a Most Champagne shippers offered their 1955 vintage *cuvées* in England in 1961, six years from the time when the grapes had been bought to make the wine.

CHAPTER THIRTEEN

Champagne Vintages
and Vintage Champagne

VINTAGE IS THE NAME given to the yearly gathering of the grapes, as harvest is the name of the gathering of the wheat. There never was a "non-vintage" year. In all the vinelands of the world, there is a vintage each year, a vintage which may be good, or poor, very good, or very bad: it all depends upon the hours of sunshine and the inches of rain which the vines enjoyed or missed during the year, not to mention frost and fogs, hail and other accidents such as bugs and fungus which can do so much damage to the vines. Thus every year do the vineyards of the world bring forth a more or less plentiful crop of grapes, the quality of which greatly varies from vintage to vintage, as does the quality of the wine made from them.

If we take the vintages of the last dozen years, from 1950 to 1961, there are a great many different Bordeaux and Burgundy wines, Hocks and Moselles, and the wines of other parts, which we could, and still can, choose from; wines that bear the date of their native vintage, any one of the past twelve years. But not Champagne. The only wines of the last twelve years which were ever offered for sale are those of the 1952, 1953 and 1955 vintages. Presently we shall be able to buy a 1959 Champagne, but it is not ready, hence not available at present. Why is this? There was Champagne made in every one of the past twelve years, much Champagne, genuine Champagne, good enough Champagne but not all of it good enough for vintage Champagne: only four years out of the twelve were able to pass the test.

Owing to their geographical position in Europe, so near the northern limit beyond which grapes cannot ripen fully more than once every three or four years, the vineyards of Champagne do not yield a crop of "vintage" quality every year. It is true that the growers of the Rhine and Moselle are no better off, but they sell their wine under the date of its native vintage, be it good, bad or indifferent. Not so the people of Champagne. Should the sun refuse to shine or the rain to stop during the summer, they do not sell the wine of that vintage as it is; it is not good enough. They blend it with wines of past and better years, purposely kept in reserve; such blends make undated or non-vintage Champagne, always a most acceptable wine and often a very nice wine indeed, although it has not the individuality of vintage Champagne.

Vintage Champagne is the wine of one year only, and, of course, of a particularly good year, and it possesses the characteristics of its native vintage. Good vintages are not all alike any more than good people are all alike, and the personality of a vintage Champagne is, to my mind, its outstanding merit. Any one of us may prefer a certain non-vintage Champagne to a particular vintage Champagne: it is a matter of taste or of luck. The non-vintage *cuvées* of all the leading Champagne shippers are good wines, some of them very good, but they are, and they are always meant to be, as much as possible the same in type and style, whereas the vintage *cuvées* of the same firms vary from vintage to vintage.

Another important difference between vintage and non-vintage Champagne, besides the difference in their relative prices, is that whilst supplies of non-vintage wines are usually assured at all times, the quantities of each vintage *cuvée* are strictly limited and one may only too easily find that a favourite vintage is "sold out" sooner than one had anticipated.

The difference between vintage and non-vintage Champagne, which is so great today, did not exist a hundred years ago. Up to the 'sixties of the last century, the wines of each vintage were sold for what they were worth, year by year, as is still the practice in Bordeaux and the Rhine. But those were the days of highly sugared Champagne, and vintage Champagne proper dates from the late 'sixties and early 'seventies, when drier wines were demanded by some of the wine-merchants of England.

At first, vintage Champagne was sold with no other guarantee than the word and good name of the seller: there was no date of vintage on either label or cork. [a] Nobody was supposed to doubt the integrity of the merchant who stated on his invoice what the wine's vintage was; nor did anybody expect to have difficulty in recognizing at first sight and taste a '74 from a '75. But human nature being what it is, some unscrupulous dealers and caterers found the temptation too great, and to the unwary they sold Champagne bearing a vintage date to which it had no right, and at prices which were not justified. Hence, evidently, the editorial which appeared in the *Wine Trade Review*, in December 1880: "We have more than once counselled our friends in the shipping trade to brand corks with the vintage of the wine, and we are pleased that since the matter was first mentioned in this Journal, some Shippers have acted on our advice . . . For the sake of fair trade and equal justice it is, however, still desirable that the branding of the age of the wine should become more general than it now is. Certain vintages . . . possess marked characteristics by which an ordinary observer may soon learn to distinguish between one or another, but other years of inferior or mediocre quality lack these distinctive features, and it is therefore advantageous, at any rate to merchants on this side of the water, that the age of the wine should be clearly denoted on the cork."

Only a few shippers branded their corks during the 'seventies, but by the 'eighties the practice had become fairly general, maybe because there were more Champagne shippers than ever before, some of whom appear to have shipped practically any wine as a vintage Champagne. From 1881 to 1891, there were but two vintages of outstanding merit – 1884 and 1889 – in spite of which there were vintage *cuvées* with branded corks of the 1883, 1885, 1886 and 1887 vintages shipped overseas, whilst non-vintage *cuvées* were still the rule on the Continent. There were quite as many vintages shipped during the last decade of the nineteenth century, and on the whole wines of better quality – the wines of 1892, 1893, 1895, 1898, 1899 and 1900 being among the best.

During the first few years of the twentieth century, the English market was fairly flooded with a succession of vintage *cuvées*, including those of 1898,

1899 and 1900, but there did not appear to be any glut, and when the fine 1904 and 1906 vintages were ready for sale, they were snapped up by the Trade in no time. Vintage Champagne was not included among trustee securities, but it was at the time a safe and highly profitable investment, besides being, of course, an excellent drink. Vintage after vintage offered to the wholesale trade in Great Britain, by the British agents of the more popular shippers, was always "over-subscribed". The more or less rapid – and sometimes spectacular – appreciation of the "script" depended upon the popularity of the brand of Champagne at the time. As soon as the wine had been "allotted", and before it had been shipped, the "script" went to a premium, and many wine-merchants advised their customers to buy a newly shipped vintage Champagne *en primeur*, before its price rose appreciably, as it invariably did in the case of the more popular brands, so that a great deal more Champagne must have been imported than was actually drunk during the first fourteen years of the present century.

Today, the greater initial cost of Champagne at the seat of production, and the very much higher rate of duty which Champagne has to pay in Great Britain and other markets, make any appreciation in its selling value practically impossible, so that there is no speculation in vintage Champagne any more. [b] Wine merchants, wholesale and retail, buy from the shipper's agents what quantities they are likely to sell from day to day, or at best from year to year, so long as stocks of each particular vintage happens to be available: also consumers buy Champagne by the bottle or by the dozen, as a drink, which it is, and no longer as an investment, which it was never meant to be.

A much simplified appraisal of the quality
of the Champagne Vintages from 1800 to 1961

o = No good   7 = The best

1800 – 3	1830 – 4	1860 – 1	1890 – 3
1801 – 2	1831 – 6	1861 – 6	1891 – 2
1802 – 7	1832 – 7	1862 – 7	1892 – 7
1803 – 6	1833 – 5	1863 – 6	1893 – 7
1804 – 7	1834 – 7	1864 – 5	1894 – 3
1805 – 1	1835 – 5	1865 – 7	1895 – 6
1806 – 6	1836 – 3	1866 – 1	1896 – 5
1807 – 5	1837 – 4	1867 – 5	1897 – 5
1808 – 4	1838 – 5	1868 – 7	1898 – 6
1809 – 2	1839 – 6	1869 – 3	1899 – 7
1810 – 6	1840 – 6	1870 – 7	1900 – 7
1811 – 7	1841 – 3	1871 – 2	1901 – 4
1812 – 2	1842 – 7	1872 – 3	1902 – 3
1813 – 3	1843 – 3	1873 – 2	1903 – 4
1814 – 2	1844 – 5	1874 – 7	1904 – 7
1815 – 2	1845 – 4	1875 – 6	1905 – 5
1816 – 1	1846 – 7	1876 – 3	1906 – 7
1817 – 2	1847 – 3	1877 – 4	1907 – 6
1818 – 7	1848 – 6	1878 – 5	1908 – 4
1819 – 7	1849 – 5	1879 – 1	1909 – 5
1820 – 4	1850 – 3	1880 – 7	1910 – 0
1821 – 1	1851 – 2	1881 – 3	1911 – 7
1822 – 7	1852 – 3	1882 – 2	1912 – 3
1823 – 3	1853 – 2	1883 – 4	1913 – 6
1824 – 2	1854 – 1	1884 – 6	1914 – 7
1825 – 7	1855 – 4	1885 – 3	1915 – 6
1826 – 5	1856 – 6	1886 – 1	1916 – 5
1827 – 4	1857 – 7	1887 – 4	1917 – 6
1828 – 6	1858 – 6	1888 – 2	1918 – 4
1829 – 3	1859 – 3	1889 – 7	1919 – 6

1920 − 7	1931 − 4	1942 − 6	1953 − 7
1921 − 7	1932 − 3	1943 − 5	1954 − 3
1922 − 3	1933 − 6	1944 − 3	1955 − 7
1923 − 7	1934 − 7	1945 − 6	1956 − 4
1924 − 5	1935 − 5	1946 − 3	1957 − 2
1925 − 5	1936 − 2	1947 − 7	1958 − 5
1926 − 7	1937 − 6	1948 − 4	1959 − 7
1927 − 3	1938 − 5	1949 − 6	1960 − 3
1928 − 7	1939 − 3	1950 − 3	1961 − 6
1929 − 7	1940 − 4	1951 − 2	
1930 − 3	1941 − 5	1952 − 7	

NOTES:

a Vintage Port was sold likewise, without any record of the vintage year on the label, and the bottles were never labelled before the present century.

b Most popular brands of vintage Champagne were sold at or below 80s. per dozen, duty paid, London, to the wholesale trade up to and including the 1900 vintage: many rose in time to a retail price of 240s., which is now far below the starting wholesale price of the latest vintage *cuvées* sold in the British Isles.

CHAPTER FOURTEEN

The Champagne Bottle

A GALLON IS A LEGAL STANDARD MEASURE for wine in the United Kingdom and in the United States.[a] It is impersonal, without any shape or colour of its own. How many people have ever seen a gallon of wine or would know that it is a gallon if they saw one? Very few. But we all know a bottle of wine when we see one: we may not be quite sure about the exact number of fluid ounces of wine there is in it. but we recognize at once its shape, size and colour, and we know exactly what kind of wine there is in it.

Today, most wine bottles are made of glass: Champagne bottles are always glass bottles. There was a time, of course, when wine bottles were made of leather, pewter, copper or silver, and they were unbreakable – the old leather "bottles" were not merely unbreakable, they were practically indestructible! There were also bottles made of plain earthenware and decorated china, and whatever the material, shape, size and look of the wine bottles of long ago, they all served the same purpose: they were containers used as decanters for wine either to be brought to the table when called for, or else to be carried far or near, slung over the shoulder or hooked on the saddle of one's horse, to slake the thirst of travellers, pilgrims, and workers in fields or anywhere away from home.

Unlike all the bottles of former ages, and many of the modern bottles as well, the Champagne bottle is and has always been the home of its wine, a real home occupied for the whole of its life, a home in which it has to grow from still to sparkling, and from immature youth to mellow maturity, from five to ten years: and sometimes to serene old age, maybe twenty years or even longer.

What is remarkable is the fact that the Champagne bottle has varied in shape, but hardly at all in contents during the past three hundred years of its existence, and that its contents have been very nearly the same as the contents of all wine bottles from the early B.C. dynasties of Egypt to the present day, in the U.S.S.R. as in the United States, in France as in Great Britain.

The legal contents of the Champagne bottle in France is 80 centilitres, equal to 27 (U.K.) fluid oz. or 46.49 cubic in., a fraction over the contents of the "reputed quart" of England, which is $2/3$ of an imperial quart, or $26^2/3$ fluid oz. (British) or 46.24 cubic in., whilst its American counterpart holds $4/5$ of the American legal quart, or 25.6 fluid oz. or 46.20 cubic in.

In Russia, the more ordinary wine bottle holds $6\frac{1}{4}$ tcharkas, or 46.91 cubic in.

The universality of the 46 cubic in. wine bottle leads one to believe that it was during all the centuries and among many different races the right and acceptable quantity of wine which an adult would drink per meal each day.

The contents of the Champagne bottle was first defined officially, as far as we have been able to trace, on March 8 1735, by an *ordonnance royale* which stipulated that sparkling wine *flacons* must weigh 25 oz. and hold as much as the *Pinte de Paris*: this was equal to 0.93 litre, not very much more than the 0.80 litre of the present Champagne bottle.[b] In 1736, Bertin du Rocheret wrote to one of his clients that his *flacons* held *une pinte*.

There were before the middle of the nineteenth century no glass-works in or near Reims, and the merchants of the Marne had to buy their bottles from the glass-works of Lorraine and Northern France. Writing about the very succesful vintages of 1834 and 1842, for instance, Max Sutaine records that he estimated the total output of all the Lorraine and Nord glass-works at from 8 to 9 million bottles a year, that is bottles of good quality suitable for Champagne, and he adds that in both years, 1834 and 1842, there was more wine to bottle than there were bottles to be bought.[c]

The shape and size of all wine bottles is important. So is the choice and quality of the various materials used in their making; and this is particularly true of Champagne bottles, which have to be heavier and stronger than other wine bottles in order to stand the strain of the *prise de mousse* and the pressure of the carbonic acid gas generated by the fermentation of the wine safely locked in, or corked in, its glass prison.

The Champagne bottle of today is made mostly of melted sand with other materials in the following proportions:-

Sand (Silica)	70 %
Carbonate of Soda	15 %
Carbonate of Lime	7 %
Manganese	2 %
Iron Oxide	2 %
Alumine	2 %
Magnesia	2 %
	100

To which it is also customary to add from 20 % to 40 % of broken glass or "cullet".

In the making of the Champagne bottle, the materials used represent barely 15 % of the total cost of production. The greatest expense of all is the constant heating of the ovens in which the bottles are baked: it represents about 45 % of the total cost, whereas the wages account for 25 %, and overheads for the remaining 15 %.

Up to 1914, Champagne bottles were hand-made, or rather man-blown: the blower gathered the molten metal in a hell-like furnace at the end of a long and hollow metal cane; he then had to blow hard until his breath parted the molten glass and pushed it out somewhat in the shape of a great, fat, burning sausage. By the time the blower was completely out of breath, he dropped the burning shapeless object, dangling at the end of his cane, into a hinged cast-iron mould with a "punt" at the bottom, and two hinged sides which closed up and gave the bottle its shape; the blower had to find more wind to stretch the metal uniformly, as he also drew up the cane to the right height of the neck of the bottle. When the blower was satisfied that all was well, the sides of the mould were opened and the red hot bottle was carried at the end of a long pole, by a young boy apprentice, to a very hot oven where it was left to bake and get really tough. This killing work went on without a break in three shifts during twenty-four hours, day and night, as the molten glass could not be allowed to cool. Glass blowers never lived long, and their lives were not insurable at anything like an acceptable premium, in spite of which there was never a shortage of men and apprentices for the glass-works, and whenever there was talk of having the Champagne bottles made by machinery, the blowers were all against it.

During the First World War most of the glass-works, where the Champagne bottles used to be made, were damaged, or destroyed, and the others had to stop working; there were no men available, and there was no coal for the ovens. After the War, a few only of the old glass blowers came back, and there had been no apprentices made to replace the men who had been killed or maimed. It made it imperative to find new techniques to supply the Champagne trade with the right quality and quantity of bottles. It was then, in 1922, that the Boucher patent bottle-making machine was introduced; each machine was worked by a single man, but there was a "mate", called *couleur*, who was responsible for feeding two machines. It was in 1924 that the Champagne trade used the machine-made bottles for the first time, the proportion of these growing year by year, so that by 1930 there were practically 50 % machine-made bottles used and 50 % hand-made or man-blown – *bouteilles mécaniques* and *bouteilles à la main* as they were called. At that time some glass-works adopted a greatly improved American machine which was not only *mécanique* but *automatique*, and it was not long before all other glass-works adopted it. By 1936, hand-made bottles had completely ceased to be made, but there were still a small proportion of *bouteilles mécaniques* made.

Since the last War, all Champagne bottles have been made by the automatic American machines capable of producing a much greater quantity of bottles, and at a lower cost. Hence, whereas there used to be some twenty glass-works to keep the Champagne trade supplied, the present much larger demand for Champagne bottles is met by three or four glass-works only, chiefly the *Société*

française Nord Verre – Verreries Charbonneaux, de Masnières et Fourmies réunies.[d]
A single automatic machine produces about 23,000 bottles per day, and one
single kiln usually serves three machines with an average output of 70,000
bottles per day.

Before 1914, the best (*premier choix*) bottles cost 36 francs per 100: in 1924,
the *à la main* bottles cost 140 post-war francs per 100, and the *mécaniques* cost
120 francs: in 1929, the *à la main* cost 200 francs and the *mécaniques* 160 francs:
in 1933, the *automatiques*, when first available, cost 125 francs, and in 1961
they cost NF. 42.56, plus 25 % tax.

The machine-made Champagne bottles not only cost much less than hand-
made bottles would cost to make today, but they are also more uniform in
quality, so much so that the loss through bursting bottles *en caves*, which averaged 5 % before 1914, is now under 1 %.[e]

Champagne bottles are heavier and stronger than all other wine bottles:
they are also better dressed. It was not always so. Up to the beginning of the
nineteenth century, the only distinction of Champagne bottles was a "cap" of
sealing wax which protected from the damp, and maybe from the rats, of Champagne cellars, the four strands of string holding the cork in position. It was
no ornament. Sometimes the Champagne shipper used sealing wax of different
colours for the wines of different vintages or vineyards. Better protection for
the cork was eventually found to be a small piece of thin lead, soon to be replaced, however, by gold or silver tin foil, applied not only to the cork but
round the whole of the neck of the bottle. This became the Champagne bottle
foil as we know it today. When it is made of various materials and in a variety
of colours, plain or speckled, distinctive and ornamental, as well as serving
the original purpose of protecting the cork. As some kind of finishing touch
to the modern foil, there is often at its base a paper band, *cravate* or collar with
a white background and either the name of the shipper and the year of the
wine's vintage are printed on it, or some such particulars are usually more
boldly displayed upon the "body label" of the bottle. This body label is the
main label and it might be called the wine's identity card. It gives in clear and
often artistically designed script the name and address of the firm responsible
for the wine which is in the bottle, that is to say the name of the shipper who
grew the grapes or bought them at the time of the vintage, who made the wine,

blended it, cared for it, and sold it, and who will be responsible for it, morally although not legally, to the day when it will be drunk, the day of the wine's glory . . . and of its death.

All kinds of other information is also given on either the body label or other small labels stuck on the bottle's shoulder or back, such as the vintage of the wine, the date of the foundation of the firm, the particular name, if any, of the wine's *cuvée*, whether the firm holds a Royal Warrant or any other such distinction, and so on. The colour of the paper of the body label may also vary with the quality or style of the wine, be it white, black, blue, yellow, gold, etc. – Carte Blanche, Carte Noire, Carte Bleue, Carte Jaune, Carte d'Or, etc.

There are also a great many bottles of Champagne, the body labels of which bear names, mostly aristocratic names, of fictitious people: they are names chosen or invented by wine-merchants, who register them so that no wine can be offered for sale under those names by competitors. The wine in the bottles is, of course, genuine Champagne bought by the wine-merchant from either a Champagne shipper or a Champagne grower, and it is the wine-merchant, not the shipper or grower, who is responsible to his customer for the quality of the wines of his choice. Such Champagnes are known in the wine trade as B.O.B. (Buyers' Own Brands).

The two sizes of Champagne bottles which are the more popular are the Bottle, or reputed quart of 80 centilitres (6 to the gallon), and the Half Bottle or reputed pint of 40 centilitres (12 to the gallon). Next comes the Magnum (3 to the gallon) which holds 2 bottles. There are still made, although not nearly to the same extent as formerly, more particularly for the British Market, the Imperial Pint of 60 centilitres (8 to the gallon), which holds half the quantity of wine in an Imperial Quart, a bottle, however, which was never used for Champagne. In Victorian times, the Imperial Pint was the ideal size for a temperate man who might consider that a bottle of Champagne with his meal was just a little more than he wanted, but who would not be satisfied with a half bottle. In all four sizes, the wine finishes fermenting in the glass, after which it is *dégorgé*, or cleared of all sediment, and *dosé*, or liqueured according to the taste of various customers in different markets, before being corked for a second and last time.

Champagne is also bottled in Quarter Bottles or Nips of 20 centilitres (24 to the gallon), a size fit only for the sick room: it holds but one glass of wine which soon loses its bubbles after the cork has been released. The Champagne in a nip or quarter bottle is never so good as that of the bottle from which it has to be decanted.

At the other end of the scale of human thirst, there is the Double Magnum, also called a Jeroboam, which holds 2 Magnums, or 4 Bottles (0.70 gallon). When the wine in a Jeroboam has been decanted from 4 bottles it is not so good, but all the better shippers are now able to handle Jeroboams in the same way as they do Magnums, so that their wine is as lively and as good as that of Magnums.

There are other bottles, larger than the Jeroboam, made for show, fully dressed but rarely filled with decanted Champagne: they are the Rehoboam, made to hold 6 Bottles; the Methuselah, 8 bottles; the Salmanezer, 12 bottles; and the Nebuchadnezzar, 20 bottles.

NOTES:

[a] In Great Britain, the basic capacity measure for wine is the imperial gallon; it was defined in 1824 (5 Geo. III 74) as the volume occupied by 10 lb. of pure water at 62 °F, which is equal to 277.42 cubic inches. Before 1824, there were three different legal gallons, the "corn" gallon of about 270 cubic in., the "ale" gallon of about 282 cubic in., and the "wine" gallon of 231 cubic in.

   In the U.S.A., all weights and measures were of English origin until 1830 when the Senate decided to fix a standard gallon and chose the Queeen Anne gallon of 231 cubic in., which is why the American legal gallon is almost exactly 5/6 of the British imperial gallon.

   In France, since the Revolution and the adoption of the metric system, the *litre*, of 100 centilitres, is the legal standard wine measure.

[b] 8 Mars 1735. 1⁰ La matière vitrifiée servant à la fabrication des bouteilles et carafons destinés à enfermer les vins et autres liqueurs, sera bien raffinée et également fondue, en sorte que chaque bouteille ou carafon soit d'une égale épaisseur dans sa circonférence.

2⁰ Chaque bouteille ou carafon contiendra à l'avenir pinte, mesure de Paris, et ne pourra être au-dessus du poids de vingt-cinq onces; les demies et quarts à proportion. Quant aux bouteilles et carafons doubles et au-dessus, ils seront aussi proportionnés à leur grandeur.

It was also stated in the same *Ordonnance* that Champagne corks must be held by a *ficelle à trois fils bien tordue et nouée en croix sur le bouchon*.

Chaptal in his *Traité historique et pratique sur la culture de la vigne avec l'art de faire le vin* (Vol. II. p. 329) wrote that it would be desirable that the rules applying to the Champagne bottles should apply to the bottles of other French wines.

c Dans les deux années que je viens de citer (1834 & 1842), les produits de toutes les verreries du Nord et de la Lorraine, qui alimentent la Champagne, ont été absorbés entièrement, et il est resté encore dans les celliers une quantité notable de vins en cercles. *Essai sur l'histoire des vins de la Champagne, par M. Max Sutaine. Reims.* 1845. p. 100.

d Monsieur G. Clignet is the Executive Director of this concern, and it is to him that we owe most of the information given above.

e One of the oddest jobs of the Champagne shippers' staff was that of the man who took delivery of the bottles bought from the glass-works: he used to take the bottles two by two from the crates, by the neck, and before stacking them away he knocked their sides to make sure that they "rang" true; if they did not, or if they broke, they were rejected.

CHAPTER FIFTEEN

Corks

OF ALL THE PROBLEMS which a Champagne shipper has to face, one of the most difficult always has been to find good corks. Corks are his best friends since they keep the wine and its gas in the bottle; Champagne never had a chance to sparkle until corks were available for use as stoppers. But many a cork has proved a false friend and has cost untold expense and annoyance, either by refusing to come out and to let the wine in the bottle come out, or by spoiling past redress the wine it was meant to keep safely.

It sometimes happens that the cork refuses to come out of the bottle, in spite of the pressure of the carbonic aced gas within and the hard tugging at its head. The best way to coax a stiff cork is to hold its head firmly in one hand and to pull away from it the punt of the bottle with the other hand. If this does not succeed, the head of the cork usually breaks off and a corkscrew has to be used. But some Champagne corks beat the best corkscrews, which may break in the cork without the cork moving a fraction of an inch. It is well to remember, when using a corkscrew to draw a stubborn Champagne cork, to wrap a serviette or thick cloth round the neck of the bottle, in case the neck

breaks and cuts one's hand. When a cork not only breaks in the neck of the
bottle, but refuses to come out with a corkscrew, the only thing to do is to hold
the bottle in the left hand well below the shoulder, and to hit one sharp blow
with the back of a carving knife from below the "ring" of the bottle-neck
outwards. When the bottles are made, the "ring" is added after the rest of the
bottle has been shaped, ánd it will usually respond and fly off when tapped
sharply away.

But such hard corks are happily of very rare occurence; whereas "corked"
and "corky" Champagne is not as exceptional as shippers and their clients would
like it to be. "Corked" Champagne, strictly speaking, means a bottle with
the cork in it, but it is popularly used in place of "corky" to mean a bottle
of Champagne which is undrinkable because its cork is bad and has tainted
it with a musty smell. Corked Champagne cannot be used for cooking, and it
must not be used for watering aspidistras or the flowers in the window boxes:
it has to be poured down the sink. Naturally all the Champagne shippers do
their very best to choose and use none but sound and perfect corks, but somehow or other some of the most beautiful-looking corks can, and do, go wrong
and stink after they have lived for a time with the wine in the bottle, just as
some of the worst blackguards on earth may have looked the sweetest little
angels once upon a time!

For many years, Champagne corks were cut from planks or boards of cork
bark from the slow growing cork-oaks growing upon some of the upper
slopes on the Spanish side of the Pyrenees. That was during the leisurely days
of long ago when cork bark was given twenty years to grow, hard and thick,
before being cut off the tree. By the beginning of the present century, cork
growers found it uneconomical to wait for a generation to grow up before getting
any dividend from their oaks, and the practice became fairly general in Spain
to strip the oak of its bark every nine or ten years. As the thickness of the
bark was only half what it has to be to make Champagne corks, the obvious
solution was to stick together two halves or pieces of cork cut lengthwise.
As there was a danger that the glue used to stick together the pieces of cork
might spoil the wine, *rondelles* or discs of the best quality cork bark and of exactly
the right diameter were stuck at the lower end of the cork, that is the end that
would be in the neck of the bottle and in contact with the wine, so that there

could not be any chance of the wine being at all tainted by the glue. As this proved to be a success, the next step was to make corks of cork-dust stuck together, no longer by hand but by machinery, with the *rondelle* at one end to keep the smell and taste of the glue well away from the wine in the bottle. The great economic benefit of this technique was that cork growers were able to use the cork bark of the cork-oaks' branches, which up to then had been of no use to them.

The first cork used when the Champagne is bottled was until recently a plain cork held by a clamp or *agrafe*, but now most shippers use a Crown cork – the beer bottle cork! The second and final cork used when the Champagne is *dégorgé* still is a "Champagne Cork" which has been bought "plain" from the cork merchants, and is branded by each shipper with his name or brand and the date of the wine's vintage for vintage wines.

CHAPTER SIXTEEN

Champagne Glasses

S PARKLING CHAMPAGNE IS SO DIFFERENT from all other wines that it has had to have a glass of its own, and it has had not one but two, the *flûte* and the *coupe*. Both glasses have known fluctuating fortunes of fashion and popularity at various times and in different countries, but both have been used for Champagne during the past three hundred years, that is from the time when sparkling Champagne was first introduced to polite Society in London, by St-Evremond, down to the present day. The *coupe*, or *tazza*, as it was first called, was designed especially for Champagne in or about 1663, whereas the *flûte*, or *tall glass*, as it was known originally, was used many years before sparkling Champagne had ever been heard of. It was first made at Murano, near Venice, in the late sixteenth century, and it was imported – and copied later on – both in the Netherlands, where it was used for Rhenish and other wines, and in England, where it was used for bottled ale, audit ale, stone ale, and other strong brews of ale.

In his "Suit or Petition to the House of Lords" (1639?), Sir R. Mansel claims that it was thanks to the Glass Patent granted to him that "Cristall beer glasses", which used to be imported from Venice and cost 20s. to 24s. per

dozen, now being home-made, cost but 10s. to 11s. per dozen. Likewise, the "Christall wine glasses", imported from Venice, used to cost 18s. per dozen but now that they were home-made, they cost 7s. to 8s. per dozen only. [a]

The difference in the price of the ale glasses and the wine glasses was obviously due to the fact that the ale glasses were the taller and better of the two. The tall glasses or *flûtes* were of two kinds, "those in which the long tapering body descends upon a bulb forming part of the stem and resting upon a moulded base and foot, after the Venetian manner, and the Low Countries 'Façon de Venise'; and those succeeding them in which the tapering *flûte* rests directly upon the foot." [b] This later kind was simpler and easier to make, and it was the first to be made in England, at the end of the seventeenth century, and in France, during the greater part of the eighteenth century.

The tall glasses or *flûtes* made in England during the eighteenth century could be used, and evidently were used, indifferently for ale and Champagne, but some of them were engraved with distinctive conventional devices such as hop bloom and ears of barley, or vine leaves and bunches of grapes, whilst there were others decorated with non-committal engraved ornaments such as

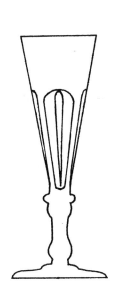

arabesques, flowers, birds, etc. The eighteenth-century decorated *flûtes* were all "made in England": the French ones were all plain, many of them made of frosted or "pearl" glass.

When sparkling Champagne was first served at the Court of Charles II and at the *petits soupers* of the most beautiful, even if not the most virtuous, of his friends, the only wine glasses available were quite useless for the new wine: their bowl was much too small and too wide open to hold the *mousse* of the wine when it was poured out, and to show off its bubbles after the glass had been filled. There was no choice: one had to use the tall ale glasses or *flûtes* which served the purpose excellently. But we can well imagine that so fastidious a man of taste as St-Evremond was not too happy to have his Champagne, so new and so aristocratic a wine at the time, served in glasses which anybody and everybody could and did use for common strong ale. There surely ought to be a new glass for Champagne, a new glass for a new wine, and a fine glass for a fine wine. As it happened, he had among his aristocratic friends the very man for the job, the Duke of Buckingham.

The Duke of Buckingham had a "glass house" at Greenwich, where he first of all made "Cristall" for Venetian looking-glasses, but having failed to secure the renewal of his Patent, when he applied for it on June 30, 1663, he turned his attention to the making of Venetian drinking glasses under Royal patronage. According to Hartshorne, the Duke had probably brought to England a company of Venetian glass makers by 1662, and there is no doubt that the tazza-shaped goblet that faces page 225 in Hartshorne's *Old English Glasses* is a remarkable ancestor of all the later Champagne *coupes*. Hartshorne describes it as an "English Glass Façon de Venise", and "an undoubted and dated example from Buckingham's glass house", adding, in a note, that it was probably presented to the King by Buckingham.

Buckingham's lead was soon followed, and Grant R. Francis[e] gives a number of illustrations of beautiful tazza-shaped Champagne glasses of the late seventeenth and early eighteenth centuries. He describes the earliest of the glasses illustrated in his book as follows: "It cannot have been made much later than 1700, and it is quite possibly a seventeenth-century specimen. The metal, albeit of the very finest, is typical of the early period in colour, texture and weight, and it has in it two of those 'blobs' of crude sand which show that its manufacture had not reached that certainty and perfection that it was so soon to attain. The design of the bowl, the beautifully proportioned baluster stem, and the curves of the domed and fluted foot, together produce a vessel of surpassing distinction and beauty, which led one of the leading experts to remark that it was the finest undoubted early champagne glass that he had ever seen."

Such glasses were very fine but they were naturally very costly as well, and judging from the very limited number of specimens which have survived to this day, they were probably used only in the houses of Queen Anne and the first two Georges, after which they ceased to be made altogether. For fully a hundred years, the *flûte* was the universally accepted Champagne glass in England as well as in France, but the old tazza-shaped Champagne glass came back into favour, in a simplified form, as the Champagne *coupe*, and it has remained in favour ever since.

As a matter of fact, both *flûte* and *coupe* are anything but ideal glasses for Champagne, the first being more suitable for a sip than a drink, and the other not giving the wine a fair chance to keep and show off its bubbles.

The best glass for Champagne is the one sponsored by the official *Comité*

Interprofessionnel du Vin de Champagne, a half-opened tulip on a tall cut-glass stem, but Champagne can be drunk with ease and pleasure out of many other wine glasses. I had, once upon a time, a dozen crystal mugs, made in Scotland, which held a pint and were great favourites with the more thirsty of my friends. Seven "stars" scratched on their bottom (the mugs' bottom) provided rough points from which the bubbles rose together vertically, quite a pretty sight, but for a very short time only!

NOTES:

a British Museum MS. 669 f.4 (7) Original Document No. XXIII in Hartshorne's *Old English Glasses*, p. 435.

b Hartshorne. *Old English Glasses*, 1897. p. 336.

c *Old English drinking glasses: their chronology and sequence.* By Grant R. Francis F.S.A. 1926. p. 89.

CHAPTER SEVENTEEN

The "Spanish Champagne" Case

by Robert Keeling

ONE SUMMER IN THE MID 1950s, an English student at Madrid University, hardly turned 21, found himself at the castle of Perelada, not far from Gerona, in the north-east of Spain, where he tasted the wines from the local vineyards. Most of them were still wines, but one was sparkling. He not only liked the sparkling wine but saw possibilities for its commercial exploitation in England. And so, towards the end of 1956, Champagne shippers in England slowly became aware of the presence of a usurper. To the long list of borrowed plumes another had been added. The long-suffering and still largely ignorant British public were being offered "Perelada Spanish Champagne".

No one successfully launches such a project without careful preparation, and "Spanish Champagne" was no exception. Discreet enquiries were made from the Customs and Excise authorities about the effect of the English law of merchandise marks; elaborate publicity material was divised; first class selling agents were sought and found. A company was formed, the Costa Brava Wine Co. Ltd, with a mixed English and Spanish board. But hardened though it was by years of "Spanish Sauternes" and "Spanish Graves", a considerable and influential part of the British wine trade found "Spanish Champagne" an affront. It was indeed the last straw. In the summer of 1957 the project was publicly attacked at a famous and fashionable wine tasting. "Perelada" replied through the wine trade press and invited anyone who did not like the new description either to hold his peace or to bring proceedings.

If the issue needed forcing, this was more than enough. Anxious consultation followed between the Association of Champagne Importers in Britain and their French counterparts, the growers and merchants in Reims and Epernay, who worked in this, as in all other communcal purposes, through the *Comité interprofessionnel du vin de Champagne* (the C.I.V.C.) at Epernay.

Nor was this all. Frenchmen take seriously their national treasures; noble wines are one of the gifts of France to the civilized world, and of all wines Frenchmen count Champagne as the crown. The French Government had long since set up an organisation to control the use of French wine names within France and to seek, if possible, to protect them from abuse abroad. This organisation, called the *Institut National des Appellations d'Origine des Vins et eaux-de-vie* (the I.N.A.O.), joined the discussions with enthusiasm, and thereafter took a major part in the battle; for it was decided to accept Perelada's challenge and go to law.

But the law was no more simple and straightforward than it usually is. On the one hand lay the Merchandise Marks Acts. To invoke these meant mounting a so-called criminal action, with the possibility of the defence electing trial by jury. The advantages lay in a fairly quick procedure and an orthodox case, well marked by legal precedent and with apparently strong chances of success; albeit with the hazard of a jury. On the other hand lay the Chancery Division of the High Court and a civil action for "passing off". In the High Court, Champagne would be legally defined by a High Court judge, and a judgment in favour of Champagne would establish a resounding precedent, far outweighing the one word "guilty" which would be the result of a successful prosecution before a jury under the Merchandise Marks Acts. But the law in such an action was difficult and involved breaking new ground and establishing new principles.

In the event, the Champagne interests chose the criminal courts, largely because the chances of success looked greater even though the prize was not so glittering; the defence, not unexpectedly, chose trial by jury rather than run the risk of a judgment of a magistrate; and so, after a preliminary skirmish before Mr Robey, the Clerkenwell magistrate, the case opened before a judge and jury in the notorious Court No. 1 at the Old Bailey on December 17, 1958.

One of the more remarkable features of any action of this kind, and one not generally known, is that the defence has to be told in advance the general line of the evidence the prosecution will call, who will be the prosecution's witnesses and what they will say. Champagne had mustered many well known names in the English trade to give evidence, including shippers, representatives of well known wholesale and retail houses, sommeliers, restaurateurs and writers. The defence, knowing the prosecution's witnesses in advance, had succeeded to a considerable extent in matching witness for witness. They too called wholesalers, retailers, barmen, writers and even a lady member of the public. Indeed the wine trade was deeply divided on this issue. Many whose trade had been built up on the imitation wines such as "Spanish Graves" and "Spanish Sauternes" feared that if the Champagne interests succeeded, a wholesale introduction of the system of *appellations contrôlées* would follow in England, with disastrous results for their business. Many, too, misunderstood the form of the action, and sympathised with this young man and his young company who were, they thought, being dragged like criminals by the Champagne interests to the Old Bailey. Many failed to understand that the prestige not only of Champagne but of the British wine trade was in the balance.

The jury were treated to the most prominent members of the bar of their day. Appearing for Champagne was Mr Geoffrey Lawrence Q.C. Facing him for Perelada was Mr Gerald Gardiner Q.C. The judge was Mr Justice McNair.

The case took six days, thirty witnesses were called (fifteen by each side), and the number of exhibits put to witnesses and shown to the jury reached fifty-nine; but the basic arguments were simple. The prosecution had to prove that, by calling their wine "Spanish Champagne", the Costa Brava Wine Company had applied a description to the wine which was either false or misleading. False in this context meant no more than "untrue". If the description was held to be false, then the defendants must be guilty. If it was not held to be false, then it was for consideration whether, though not false, it was misleading.

Misleading meant, as the judge explained to the jury, a statement with a catch in it. He reminded them that often a misleading statement is more dangerous than a false one.

The prosecution said that "Spanish Champagne" was false because Champagne in England meant the sparkling wine from the French province and nothing else. It was, one witness said, as French as the Folies Bergères. Therefore because "Spanish Champagne" suggested that the wine was "Champagne from Spain", it was a lie. On the misleading point, the prosecution relied on a famous precedent in a case about "British Tarragona" [a] and claimed that to argue that no one would be deceived was to assume too much knowledge on the part of the purchaser. In the British Tarragona case, it was argued by the sellers that the expression was a contradiction in terms, and that therefore it was absurd to suppose that anyone could be deceived into thinking that the wine came from Tarragona; but this argument failed because it was held that it assumed too great a degree of knowledge on the part of the purchaser.

The defence denied that "Spanish Champagne" was a lie. Champagne by itself no doubt meant what the prosecution said it meant; but when it was prefixed by the word "Spanish", it clearly meant a wine of champagne type made in Spain. Not only was it not a lie, but it deceived no one, and was a convenient expression both for trade and public. For years the British wine trade had used expressions of this kind; and Mr Gerald Gardiner gradually covered the very large table in the well of the court, used to receiving quite a different kind of criminal exhibit, with example after example of wines with mixed-up names ranging from Spanish Sauternes and Australian Burgundy to Palestinian Alicante and Chilean Barsac. If the practice is so widespread for other wines, he said, why can it not apply to Champagne, as it did, for instance, in America? The prosecution tried, but apparently in vain, to differentiate between Champagne and these other wines by calling evidence to show that the name "Champagne" had never, like those of other wines, been degraded by an alien, geographical adjective. The whole purpose of the prosecution, it was argued, was to prevent this degradation. Indeed, so far from being Champagne, Perelada was not even produced by the famous Champagne method of double fermentation in bottle. It was produced (and this was admitted) by the so-called tank method, whereby the second fermentation takes place in a huge glass-lined tank and the whole process, instead of taking years, is finished in a few weeks.

The judge's summing-up gave little comfort to the defence. He asked the jury to consider the meaning of Champagne in England only, and not to concern themselves with what it meant elsewhere. He warned the jury against the defence's argument that the word "Spanish" made it perfectly clear that the wine was not Champagne in the limited sense but something different, and he referred the jury to a case about non-brewed vinegar.[b] In this case, it was found that the essential feature of vinegar was that it was a natural product produced by fermentation. The product called "non-brewed vinegar", on the other hand, was a synthetic concoction. It was held that because vinegar is essentially a brewed product, to qualify the word "vinegar" with the word "non-brewed" was a false trade description. The judge observed that the case seemed to suggest that you cannot take a noun with a well-known meaning, add to it an adjective inconsistent with that meaning, and then say "well, taking the two together, they are not false; they are true."

Just before 3 o'clock, the jury retired, taking with them a bottle or two out of the many exhibits (for reflection rather than refreshment), and the opposing side waited with such patience as they could muster for the verdict. At a quarter to four the jury returned and found the defendants not guilty. The judge said that it was a proper prosecution to bring and a proper case for enquiry, but made the prosecution pay the defendants' costs.

The case had attracted wide publicity in the English and Continental press; "Champagne v. Spain", *The Times* called it, and thus demonstrated a nice regard for the geographical significance of Champagne. The victors naturally took every means open to them to exploit their success. Indeed, so far as much of the English press was concerned, it appeared a popular win. The young English David had triumphed against the French Goliath. The common man and his common sense had routed the pedants and the wine snobs. (Nobody seemed to notice that the principal shareholder in the Costa Brava Wine Company was reputed to be one of the richest men in Spain or that the meaning of Champagne in England seemed unaccountably to have changed overnight.) But the more serious English dailies and weeklies found the verdict disquieting, and there were suggestions that it was time the wine trade put its house in order.

The French press uttered a roar of pained and indignant surprise. Anglo-French political relations were already at an unusually low ebb. The six Common Market countries, including France, were about to start operating in January, 1959, as an exclusive trading bloc; the United Kingdom was at the head of the rival European Free Trade Area. Guinea had just elected to withdraw from the French Community and link herself to Ghana, a member of the British Commonwealth; and now "Spanish Champagne" was flooding into England, the most important foreign market for Champagne. Irritated as they already were with England and the devious ways of British politics, Frenchmen did not find it difficult to believe that somehow the British Government could have intervened in the Champagne case but deliberately chose not to as part of a general plan to embarrass France. Some bars in Paris refused for a time to sell Scotch Whisky; and a consignment of "Spanish Champagne" on its way to England was turned back by the French authorities on the Pyrenees frontier. In England questions were asked in the House of Commons by francophile M.P.s about the possibility of special protection for Champagne, but the answers were non-committal and guarded.

Then, at least as far as British comment was concerned, public discussion was brought abruptly to an end by the announcement that twelve famous Champagne houses had issued a writ against the Costa Brava Wine Company in the Chancery Division of the High Court. The Champagne interests had been quick to realise that if nothing was done to repair the damage of the Old Bailey verdict, there might be an avalanche of spurious Champagnes on sale in England from wine-producing countries all over the world, and that Champagne might quickly become only a synonym for "sparkling wine" without any geographical significance at all. So again they went back to the law to see if a High Court judge would give them the remedy under the general common law of England which a jury had failed to give them under the criminal law.

The new action needed courage. Having chosen what appeared to have been the easier path via the Old Bailey and having failed to break through, the Champagne interests were now attempting the more ambitious step of obtaining an injunction to restrain the sale of "Spanish Champagne" on the ground that this was "passing off" as Champagne a wine which was not Champagne, and therefore amounted to unfair competition. Not unexpectedly Perelada met this attack by asserting that this kind of action was unknown in English law, and that even if everything which the Champagne interests said about Champagne was assumed in the plaintiffs' favour, no actionable wrong was disclosed. It was well known, they argued, that a trader could, and often did, bring successful proceedings to protect his own name from use by a rival trader because he could show he had the goodwill in that name. But this was not a case of Bollinger bringing an action against someone selling "Spanish Bollinger". That would be a normal passing-off action and would, at least, be properly constituted. This was an action brought by Bollinger and eleven other French houses, who claimed to represent all exporters of Champagne from France to England (and who were in fact the twelve houses exporting the greatest quantity of Champagne to England) to establish that collectively and exclusively they owned not the individual rights to their own names, but the right to the name "Champagne". The defendants maintained that this kind of collective right to a geographical name might hold water under some Continental legal systems, but did not exist in England; and they sought to have the case dismissed without looking further into the particular facts alleged by the plaintiffs.

The judge agreed to try this point of law separately as a preliminary issue, on the ground that, if Costa Brava were right, there was the end of the matter, the main case would never have to be heard, and much time and money would be saved. Accordingly a long legal battle took place in November 1959 before Mr Justice Danckwerts between Mr Richard Wilberforce Q.C. (now Mr Justice Wilberforce) for the Champagne houses and Sir Milner Holland Q.C. for Costa Brava. Champagne was scarcely mentioned throughout the five day hearing. It was an exceedingly specialised discussion on the nature of the actionable wrong of passing-off in English law and, not unnaturally, was scarcely noticed in the press. But it was in fact the hinge of the whole affair. Mr Wilberforce addressed the judge for two days, a dry, refined and brilliantly annotated address, reviewing a great range of cases and offering the judge a grain or two of argument from each to show that the English common law, looked at as a whole, did not exclude the kind of protection the Champagne interests were seeking, and that indeed it was no more than a logical extension of a principle which, in previous cases, had long been recognised. He capped his argument with a bold invitation to the judge to apply the reasoning in a recent American case concerned with Minnesota flour where a group of Minnesota flour manufacturers had successfully restrained a miller outside the Minnesota District from calling his flour Minnesota flour.[c] In spite of a tremendous (and even lengthier) attempt by the defendants to discredit this argument and the cases cited in support of it, the judge found that the Champagne interests had a right in law to protect the name "Champagne" as against anyone making wine outside the Champagne district; but he hastened to make it clear that this did not decide the case in favour of the plaintiffs as they still had to prove the facts that they were asserting about Champagne. In particular his decision had no effect on the question of whether "Spanish Champagne" was likely to deceive.

But though the law was now established, the facts were still not easy, and confidence in the Spanish camp remained high. It was not enough in the Chancery Division to say, "it is a lie." What had also now to be proved was that there was a reasonable chance of someone who bought a bottle called "Spanish Champagne" being deceived by this description into thinking he was buying Champagne. At this point, the Champagne houses turned again to Mr Geoffrey Lawrence. New witnesses were interviewed, new documentary evidence was prepared, researches were made into the files of I.N.A.O. and C.I.V.C. to see what abuses there had been in the past and what action had been taken; and a note was prepared of the history of the development of Champagne both as a geographical province of France and as a wine, to show the meticulous care with which the French protected the name not only against foreign users but against makers of sparkling wines in other districts of France.

By November 1960 the formal preliminary steps had all been completed. Both sides took their taxi-loads of papers to the court, booked themselves private rooms in the courts to accomodate these and their witnesses (a procedure reserved for long and what lawyers call "heavy cases") and dug themselves in for a long siege. The final struggle – the French press later described it a little fancifully as "the Second Battle of the Marne" – opened again before Mr Justice Danckwerts on the November 29, 1960.

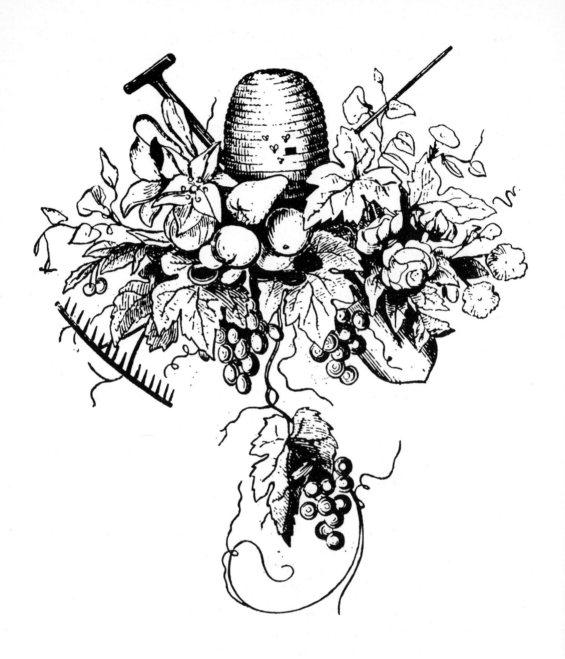

So, just two years after the Old Bailey trial, Mr Geoffrey Lawrence again opened for Champagne. The Champagne houses had to succeed in convincing the judge that Champagne had an exclusive and non-generic meaning and a high reputation; and that there was a real risk that, by describing their Spanish wine as Spanish Champagne, the defendants might mislead the more uninformed section of the public into thinking that Champagne could come from Spain. It was not difficult to prove the exclusive meaning or the high reputation but to prove likelihood of deception was far from easy.

As at the Old Bailey, the defendants argued from "Spanish Sauternes" and other names of this kind that this practice was convenient and not unknown even as applied to Champagne. Erskine Childers' famous novel *The Riddle of the Sands*, published early this century, mentioned "German Champagne"; and there were other examples of this in a few old advertisements; there had been many recent references in the press to "Russian Champagne" and one to "Persian Champagne". Even in France, a recent press report, describing a wine served at a banquet, had said "the Champagne was German". All these and other examples were patiently put to the plaintiffs' witnesses by Sir Milner Holland; newspaper after newspaper was produced – but no bottles, because no one could produce anything on sale in England and described as Champagne except Perelada and the wine from the Champagne province. Old arguments about Cheddar cheese (on the basis that "Canadian Cheddar" equals "Spanish Champagne") which had been put to some effect at the old Bailey, were put again in cross-examination. Later on in the case, the judge gave his view of these. Cheese, he observed, seemed to be as different from wine as from chalk.

But a certain unease settled upon the plaintiffs under what was a very sustained and penetrating cross-examination; indeed in this kind of case cross-examination is easier and therefore tends to be more effective than the examination by a witness's own counsel. The leading and loaded question must be answered under cross-examination; in examination-in-chief no lead can be given to the witness and he must make his own way with questions which are necessarily not always easy.

After calling twenty-one witnesses, the plaintiffs ended their case, a little dented here and there, but largely intact and with a great weight of authoritative and frank answers to support their main contentions that never had this happened to Champagne before; that Champagne occupied a unique prestige position, but that many people, particularly those with new money and developing tastes did not know where it came from; that these people seeing the word "Spanish Champagne" would easily come to think that Champagne was made in Spain. Some answers were more uncompromising than others. "No geographical description is legitimately generic in character", said one witness, and the Frenchmen in court glowed with a kind of wistful pleasure at hearing an Englishman express an opinion so at variance with much of the practice of the English wine trade. But had the witnesses sufficiently established that the public was as ignorant as the plaintiffs said? Was it really a fact that a significant section of the public really did not know – not that Champagne came from a province in France historically called Champagne – but from France at all? At least one witness thought so beyond any doubt, and he came from industrial Wales. His customers knew it simply as "the stuff they throw against ships". But the cross-examination had been powerful. The practice in the English wine trade of abusing geographical names had been regretfully admitted by the plaintiffs' witnesses; and of course none of the expert witnesses (and they were all experts) was in any danger of himself being deceived. All they could say or suggest was that in general the public was not well informed about wine. It was a matter of argument whether this would result in deception.

Then it was the defendants' turn to call their evidence. A few – very few – opening questions from Sir Milner Holland; and then the defendants' witnesses were exposed to Mr Lawrence's cross-examination. In substance, the defendants' argument was based on the simple proposition that the word "Spanish" showed that the wine did not come from France, and so "Spanish Champagne" could not be mistaken for Champagne from France. There might be a few excessively ignorant persons who might be deceived, said the defendants, but if they existed at all, they were so few and so exceptional as to be insignificant.

Nevertheless the fact remained that Spanish Champagne was not "Champagne" and the defendants' own witnesses found themselves at once in the greatest difficulty when cross-examined on this point. One witness agreed that to call it "Champagne" rather than "White Sparkling Wine" made it more attractive to the public; another said it was called a "Champagne" because it had the same characteristics and as the real Champagne. (This, of course, ran counter to the great weight of evidence which had been given that Champagne in England had not, until the appearance of Perelada, been used generically.) Another admitted that since the Old Bailey decision his wine list had omitted the word "Champagne" from the description of Perelada.

Then, when only four witnesses had been called, suddenly and unexpectedly the defendants' case came to an end and Sir Milner Holland was on his feet making his closing speech. No one had come forward for the Costa Brava Wine Company; the long procession of witnesses who had appeared at the Old Bailey had shrunk to four, and of these one lived in Scotland, and the judge did not appear disposed to consider his evidence anyhow.

The speech for the defendants lasted from the morning of December 5 until the afternoon of the following day. It developed the points already made in cross-examination and launched a powerful attack on the plaintiffs' point that a substantial section of the public could be deceived. The judge heard it with scarcely any interruption; and when at length Mr Lawrence rose to his feet for the last time, the match still looked fairly open.

The final speech started quietly; then all at once the judge seemed to be asking questions, almost for the first time in the case, and at first a little uncomfortably for the plaintiffs. "Am I right in thinking there is no evidence whatever of anyone having asked for Champagne and having been sold Spanish Champagne?" Perelada enjoyed hearing the reply. "Put that way I think your Lordship is right." Mr Lawrence then reminded the judge of certain wine lists where "Perelada Spanish Champagne" was listed among the Champagnes. But this was brushed aside. "How far", said the judge, "would the defendants be responsible for that." But then there was a further exchange which gave Mr Lawrence the unmistakable whiff of victory. The judge posed an imaginary situation where some ignorant person orders Champagne, but says to the waiter that it is rather expensive. If, said the judge, the waiter then offered Perelada, would he not add, "but of course that is not French Champagne." This was the heart of the case and Mr Lawrence saw and took his chance. "My Lord, if he said 'Not *French* Champagne', he would mean 'it is not French Champagne it is Spanish Champagne, but whether you have French Champagne or Spanish it is still Champagne'." Counsel took this further in his answer to the judge's next question: "Spanish Champagne", said Mr Lawrence, "is likely to deceive the uninformed section of the public into thinking not that they are drinking the plaintiffs' goods, because that is not this form of action, but that they are drinking *a* Champagne which can, contrary to their sort of vague ideas in the past, come from Spain." At last the corner had been turned. "I think" replied Mr Justice Danckwerts, "your argument is supported by the menu –" and he referred to a menu put in evidence where Perelada was described simply as "Champagne (Perelada)".

Mr Lawrence evidently decided it was now safe to hit about him with increasing vigour. He referred to the "utterly disastrous answers" of the defence witnesses. "I was at a party", said one witness, "and I supplied the Champagne." Plainly, in the context, commented counsel, this was Spanish Wine. "Yes", said the judge. He referred to the "generic argument" and to the strenuous attempts of the defendants to show that Champagne had previously been used in England in conjunction with an alien geographical adjective. But in spite of all their efforts, it was a very tiny mouse indeed that in the end appeared – a book in 1873, an advertisement in 1888, a novel in 1902 and a few "journalistic inaccuracies". The judge seemed disposed to agree. "And German Champagne is of course forbidden by treaty," he commented, "and 'Australian Champagne' seems to have been discontinued." In fact there had never been any clear evidence that anything called "Australian Champagne" had ever been sold in England: but Mr Lawrence presumably thought that he had the judge sufficiently with him to pass to his last and most telling point.

Perelada had published a brochure, tricked out in pink and blue, and called "Giving a Champagne Party". This contained the plaintiffs' best evidence of the tendency to drop the adjective and concentrate on the noun, and so of the tendency to deceive; Mr Lawrence had put it briefly to two witnesses, and he now let none of it escape. If he needed any encouragement, he quickly got it. "On its face", said the judge, after a few preliminary comments by counsel, "it is quite plainly intended to cash in on the reputation of Champagne." Mr Lawrence respectfully agreed and did a little underlining. "A more wicked piece of propaganda, in the sense that it cuts into the plaintiffs' goodwill, it would be difficult to imagine. Attention is focused on what is the mischievous, deceptive and misleading part of the defendants' description. This is a document which patently and blatantly sets out to pass off the defendants' product as and for Champagne. Furthermore not only does the pamphlet tempt retailers (as the defendants' own evidence had shown) to sell Perelada as and for Champagne, but it tempts the public to buy it for Champagne occasions."

Having delivered this final broadside, Mr Lawrence sat down and there were probably few who did not think that the Perelada ship was sunk. The long hearing was over, after seven days of evidence and argument; the French returned to Paris and Epernay, and the case remained suspended for a fortnight while the judge composed his judgment.

On the December 16, 1960 Mr Justice Danckwerts read his judgment. He granted the Champagne houses their injunction restraining the Costa Brava Wine Company from selling Perelada under any name which included the word Champagne. He found that what the company had done had been dishonest trading, and he ordered them to change all their labels within 48 hours so as to obliterate all mention of the word Champagne. No appeal was entered against the judgment.

Champagne thus achieved a unique position in England. Not only was this victory a great commercial success for Champagne, but its repercussions in the wine trade were considerable. Many hoped that this judgment would give encouragement to those in the newer wine producing countries to establish their own goodwill with their own regional names. Certainly to the Champenois, those stouthearted Frenchmen, and their French and English friends and colleagues, the British wine trade owed a considerable debt.

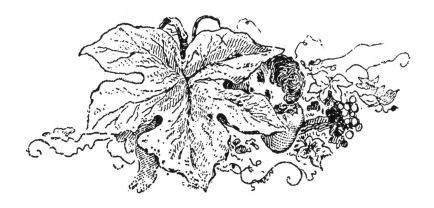

The corks popped loud in celebration and the *mousse* was the *mousse* of Champagne.

NOTES:

[a] Holmes-v-Pipers Ltd. (1914) I K.B. 57.
[b] Kat-v-Diment (1951) I K.B. 34.
[c] Pilsbury-Washburn Flour Mills Co. Ltd v Eagle (1898) 86 Fed. Rep 608.
[d] Port and Madeira are protected by treaty, but not so fully. This "post type" is permissible.

Appendices

Bibliography

Index

APPENDIX ONE

Export and Home Sales of Champagne from 1861 to 1960

1. Sales of Champagne and other Sparkling Wines — April 1861 to April 1911

Years, from April to April	Number of bottles exported	Number of bottles sold in France	Total number of bottles sold
1861-1862	6,904,915	2,592,875	9,497,790
1862-1863	7,937,836	2,767,371	10,705,207
1863-1864	9,851,138	2,934,996	12,786,134
1864-1865	9,101,441	2,801,626	11,903,067
1865-1866	10,413,455	2,782,777	13,196,132
1866-1867	10,283,886	3,218,343	13,502,229
1867-1868	10,876,585	2,924,268	13,800,853
1868-1869	12,810,194	3,104,496	15,914,690
1869-1870	13,858,839	3,688,461	17,487,300
1870-1871	7,544,323	1,633,941	9,178,264
1871-1872	17,001,124	3,367,537	20,368,661
1872-1873	18,917,779	3,464,059	22,381,838
1873-1874	18,106,310	2,491,759	20,598,069
1874-1875	15,318,345	3,517,182	18,835,527
1875-1876	16,705,719	2,439,763	19,145,481
1876-1877	15,882,964	3,127,991	19,010,955
1877-1878	15,711,651	2,450,983	18,162,634
1878-1879	14,844,181	2,596,356	17,440,537
1879-1880	16,524,593	2,666,561	19,191,154
1880-1881	18,220,980	2,399,924	20,620,904
1881-1882	17,671,366	3,190,869	20,862,235
1882-1883	17,642,821	2,869,231	20,512,052
1883-1884	18,206,956	2,675,578	20,882,534

Years, from April to April	Number of bottles exported	Number of bottles sold in France	Total number of bottles sold
1884-1885	18,189,256	2,822,601	21,011,857
1885-1886	14,923,490	2,752,184	17,675,674
1886-1887	16,222,903	2,861,971	19,984,874
1887-1888	17,257,685	3,076,639	20,334,324
1888-1889	18,904,469	3,653,615	22,558,084
1889-1890	19,148,382	1,176,189	20,526,371
1890-1891	21,699,111	4,077,083	25,776,194
1891-1892	19,685,115	4,558,881	24,243,996
1892-1893	16,600,678	4,487,535	21,088,213
1893-1894	17,359,349	4,376,518	22,235,867
1894-1895	16,129,374	4,908,281	21,037,655
1895-1896	17,966,840	6,865,845	24,832,685
1896-1897	22,855,798	6,704,115	29,559,913
1897-1898	21,697,188	5,690,599	27,387,787
1898-1899	20,988,343	8,370,570	29,358,914
1899-1900	21,773,513	6,680,923	28,454,436
1900-1901	20,628,251	7,426,794	28,055,045
1901-1902	20,311,228	7,894,212	28,205,440
1902-1903	22,523,746	9,335,412	31,859,158
1903-1904	21,084,881	9,808,774	30,493,655
1904-1905	19,845,852	8,864,947	28,710,799
1905-1906	23,876,731	11,714,404	35,591,135
1906-1907	23,056,847	10,114,548	33,171,395
1907-1908	22,212,346	11,522,272	33,734,618
1908-1909	19,992,314	12,713,024	32,705,338
1909-1910	26,173,580	13,120,946	39,294,526
1910-1911	23,066,523	15,517,879	38,584,402

2. Sales of Champagne only — 1911 to 1940

1911-1912	20,288,963	9,084,936	29,373,899
1912-1913	20,946,534	9,151,110	30,007,044
1913-1914	18,410,436	8,134,196	26,544,632
1914-1915	7,235,177	3,126,833	10,362,010
1915-1916	6,725,159	4,680,398	11,405,557
1916-1917	8,436,214	7,565,602	16,001,816
1917-1918	6,936,618	10,679,116	17,615,734
1918-1919	5,067,671	10,687,628	15,755,299
1919-1920	13,582,381	9,433,636	23,016,017
1920-1921	12,746,808	8,361,571	21,108,379
1921-1922	6,659,496	5,884,377	12,543,873
1922-1923	9,078,383	9,465,717	18,544,100
1923-1924	14,072,407	17,877,017	31,949,474

Years, from April to April	Number of bottles exported	Number of bottles sold in France	Total number of bottles sold
1924-1925	14,685,604	15,514,036	30,199,640
1925-1926	15,629,408	20,537,877	36,167,285
1926-1927	14,688,853	17,527,436	32,216,289
1927-1928	13,046,690	8,169,248	21,215,938
1928-1929	12,513,670	11,307,691	23,821,361
1929-1930	14,238,159	13,146,057	27,384,216
1930-1931	9,419,415	15,207,429	24,626,844
1931-1932	6,603,448	16,328,524	22,841,972
1932-1933	4,370,667	20,902,169	25,472,836
1933-1934	8,466,325	21,961,249	30,427,574
1934-1935	7,377,526	20,302,324	27,679,850
1935-1936	7,854,962	25,327,283	33,182,245
1936-1937	11,735,287	28,297,501	40,032,788
1937-1938	11,957,420	23,772,427	35,729,847
1938-1939	10,149,673	21,610,935	31,820,608
1939-1940	10,680,122	17,003,788	27,683,910

3. Sales of Champagne only — 1946 to 1960

Years, from April to April	Number of bottles exported	Number of bottles sold in France	Total number of bottles sold
1946-1947	11,869,422	11,235,420	23,105,042
1947-1948	10,250,976	18,864,220	29,115,194
1948-1949	11,041,034	18,240,602	29,281,636
1949-1950	13,960,362	19,439,113	33,399,475
1950-1951	15,507,436	20,750,839	36,258,274
1951-1952	12,076,452	18,651,060	30,727,512
1952-1953	11,100,079	19,477,929	30,578,008
1953-1954	11,332,272	22,153,428	33,485,700
1954-1955	12,337,560	25,773,214	38,110,774
1955-1956	13,165,588	31,278,718	34,444,306
1956-1957	12,737,100	35,705,008	48,442,108
1957-1958	13,114,937	27,787,354	40,321,308
1958-1959	13,538,957	28,731,116	42,270,083
1959-1960	13,908,922	35,356,579	49,265,501

APPENDIX TWO

The Cost per Gallon New Wine at Vintage Time before the Nineteenth Century

Approximately Converted into Shillings and Pence of Today

1555	2s.	od.	1693	22s.	6d.	1768	4s.	1d.
1569	3s.	3½d.	1694	22s.	4d.	1770	6s.	2d.
1570		6½d.	1695		7½d.	1773	4s.	1d.
1576	1s.	9d.	1700	12s.	10d.	1780	2s.	od.
1585		8¾d.	1708	4s.	6d.	1781	2s.	6d.
1587	4s.	7d.	1711	9s.	od.	1782	2s.	2d.
1592	1s.	10d.	1712	2s.	4d.	1785	2s.	od.
1602	1s.	3d.	1719		5½d.	1786	2s.	6d.
1607	4s.	2d.	1725		8d.	1787	2s.	2d.
1609	5s.	4d.	1734	9s.	4d.	1788	6s.	3d.
1610	1s.	2d.	1739	4s.	2d.	1789	1s.	8d.
1613	2s.	4d.	1740	3s.	2d.	1791	3s.	2d.
1623	3s.	od.	1743	2s.	5d.	1792	2s.	3d.
1643	3s.	4d.	1745	10s.	7d.	1793	5s.	2d.
1653	1s.	5d.	1748	2s.	1d.	1794	9s.	8d.
1664	1s.	9d.	1750	1s.	4d.	1795	1s.	6d.
1667		10½d.	1754	6s.	6d.	1796	3s.	od.
1673		3½d.	1760		7½d.	1797	2s.	6d.
1676	1s.	1d.	1762	14s.	6d.	1798	2s.	7d.
1677		1½d.	1765	1s.	6d.	1799	1s.	9d.

APPENDIX THREE

Champagne Shippers in 1862

Reims

Association Vinicole de la
  Champagne, L. Jaunay & Co
Bernard, F. & Co
Binet fils
Boden aîné
Burchard-Delbeck & Co
Châtelain, C., de Montigny & Co
Clicquot, E.
Clicquot, H.
Couvert, successor to E. Forest
Farrc, Ch.
Fisse, Thirion & Co
Forest-Fourneaux, père et fils
  (now Taittinger)
Frissard, père et fils
Gibert, G.
Gigot, Alex
Gondelle, E.
Goulet, George & Co
Goulet, N. & H

Grouselle fils
Heidsieck & Co
Heidsieck, Charles & Co
Irroy, Ernest
Krug & Co.
Lanson, père et fils
Lelegard, A.
Loche, Ch.
Lossy (de) & Co
Manuel & Co
Minet, Jeune & Boom
Moreau, A., fils aîné
Morizet-Heut
Mumm, Jules & Co
Mumm, G. H. & Co
Ohaus, F.
Piper, H. & Co
Pommery, Veuve et fils
Rivart, C.
Roederer, L.

Roederer, Thésophile & Co
Ruinart, père et fils
Ruinart, Paul & Kurz
Saint-Marceaux, (de) & Co
Schoyer-Dorlodot
Soyez, Auguste, fils & Co

Sutaine (Veuve) Max & Co
Tassigny (de) o. et Co
Walther, J. H.
Werlé & Co., successors to
    Veuve Clicquot-Ponsardin

Epernay

Charles Abelé
Bremont Bardoux
Martin Boizel
Chanoine frères
Chaurey Jaune
Chausson frères
De Venoge & Co
A. Dutemple
Jules Fournier
St-Wallon de Lochet & Co
Veuve Locquard & Ch. Choque
L. I. Luquet & Co
Méchin Martin

Eugène Mercier
Meunier, frères
Moët & Chandon
Perrier Jouët & Co
Pétrot Bonnet & Co
Thiercelin Pissard
L. Plomb
Pol Roger & Co
Alfred Roger
J. Roussillon & Co
V. Sosthène Thomas
Wachter & Co

Châlons

Benjamin & Eugène Perrier
Bullot
Adolphe Collin
Dagonet et fils
Dailzon et Lesage
Freminet et fils
J. Georg & Co

Eugène Grognot
Jacquesson et fils
Joseph Perrier, fils et Co
Lecat Lequed
Bertin Pithois
Rollett Soudant

Canton d'Ay

Aubert & fils
Alfred Aubert
Aubert & Brugnon
Ayala Albrecht
Simon Bertault
Jaillot Basserat
Riché-Bin, Ed.
Bertault Blondeau
Bollinger-de-Villermont
Jules Camuset
Henri Couvreur
Deutz & Geldermann
Taverne Duminy
Folliet, F. Duvernet,
   Scheck & Co.
Parisot Foureaux
Robinet Gondrecourt
Moreau-Gustave
Renault Hazart

Gustave Janet
Billiet Lahaye
Pinchon Lefébure
Blanchard Louis
Le Comte de Mareuil
Victor Padie
Bornot Phillipponat
Pottelain
Léon Pottelain
Brézol Robinet
Robinet de Fontenille
Guyard Robinet
Marignier Roulet
Gaspard Testulat
Vidal Tirode
Léon Vautrin
Vautrin père et fils
Walch & Co

Mareuil-sur-Ay

Moignon Alise, fils & Co
Emile Batillet & Véry
Salmon Billecart Bouche,
   fils & Co
Foucher Bruch & Co
V. Foucher, Olivier & Co
Pagin François
Saturnin Irroy

Pivin Labbey
Ch. Gaudon Malotet
Testulat Malotet
Hadot Mayeur
Alfred de Montebello & Co
Bruch Renault
A. Verrier
Hazart Verev

Avize

A. Arnoult
Henri Aubert
Augé Colin
Charles de Cazenove
Desbordes père
Dinet, fils & Co
Perruchot Doerr
Ducognon
Ch. Francart & Co
Giesler & Co
Guizet
F. Jacoby
Jouron
Koch fils

Labouré jeune
Leon Le Brun
Lecureux & Lefournier
Lefournier jeune
Marchand Révelard
H. Moré
Grandjean Planckaert
A. Puisart
Lecler Révélard
August Soulés
Verron Varnier
Lafont Vincent
Bara Vix

Percentage of the Liqueuring of Champagne: F

A composite Chart made from

twelve of the more i

	1861-65	1866-70	1871-75	1876-80	1881-85	1886-90	1891-95	96-1900	1901-05
Dosages									
15/20	10 %	5 %							
12½	15 %	10 %	10 %	5 %					
10	17 %	33 %	33 %	33 %	30 %	30 %	25 %	25 %	25 %
7½	20 %	12 %							
5	33 %	25 %	42 %	47 %	50 %	45 %	45 %	33 %	33 %
2½-3	5 %	15 %	15 %	15 %	15 %	10 %	10 %	17 %	17 %
1½-2					5 %	10 %	10 %	10 %	10 %
1						5 %	5 %	5 %	
¾									10 %
½							5 %	5 %	3 %
¼									
0								5 %	2 %

FOUR

Demi-Sec, Sec, Extra Sec, Nature or Brut

figures based on those supplied by
Champagne Shippers

1911-15	1916-20	1921-25	1926-30	1931-35	1936-40	1941-45	1946-50	1951-55	1956-60
20 %	20 %	20 %	20 %	20 %	15 %	15 %	15 %	22 %	25 %
40 %	30 %	30 %	30 %	30 %	35 %	35 %	30 %	35 %	35 %
10 %	15 %	15 %	10 %	15 %	10 %				
15 %	10 %	10 %	10 %	15 %	15 %	10 %	30 %	18 %	15 %
10 %	15 %	10 %	20 %		15 %	25 %	10 %	10 %	$12\frac{1}{2}$ %
5 %									5 %
	10 %	10 %	10 %	10 %	10 %	15 %	10 %	8 %	5 %
		5 %		10 %					
							5 %	7 %	$2\frac{1}{2}$ %

Bibliography

1. 1518 J. S. BREWER *Letters and Papers, foreign and domestic, of the reign of Henry VIII,* preserved in the Public Record Office, London, 1862-1876 Vol. 2 Part 2 No. 4581

2. 1535 *Archives municipales de Châlons-sur-Marne* BB 8 fol. 20

3. 1537 Archives nationales J. 962 No. 41 *Catalogue des actes de François Ier* Paris, 1887-1908 T. 8 No. 31674

4. 1583 CHARLES ESTIENNE ET JEAN LIÉBAULT *L'Agriculture et maison rustique* Lyon fol. 322, recto

5. 1589 JULIEN DE PAULMIER *Traité du vin et du cidre* Traduit par Jacques Chaignes Caen

6. 1600 OLIVIER DE SERRES *Le Théatre d'agriculture et ménage des champs*

7. 1622 TOBIAS VENNER *Via recta ad vitam longam* London p.28

8. 1622 *De salubri potu dissertatio* Rome cap. XXI

9. 1642 *Placcart du Roy nostre Sire sur l'entrée des vins d'Ay et aultres de charroy* Bruxelles

10. 1658 CHARLES ESTIENNE *L'Agriculture et maison rustique* p.588

11. 1667 Bibliothèque Nationale *Manuscrits français* fol. 29, 36

12. 1675 GERVASE MARKHAME *The English Housewife* p.184

13. 1688-1742 *The Diary of John Hervey, First Earl of Bristol, with Extracts of his Book of Expenses* Wells 1894

14. 1696 GEO HARTMAN *The Family Physitian* pp.471/3

15. 1709-1782 *Journal de Dom Pierre Chastelain, Bénédictin rémois* Publié sur les documents originaux de la Bibliothèque de Reims par Henri Jadart Reims, Michaud 1902

16. 1712 *Recueil de poésies latines et françaises sur les vins de Champagne et de Bourgogne* Paris

17. 1744 BERTIN DU ROCHERET *Journal des Etats tenus à Vitry le François en 1744* Châlons-sur-Marne n.d.

18. Bibliothèque d'Epernay *Manuscrits Bertin du Rocheret* T.I. p.838

19. 1775 SIR EDWARD BARRY *Observations historical and medical on the wines of the Ancients and the analogy between them and modern wines* Appendix pp.8425/6

20. 1777 *Question traitée dans les Ecoles de la Faculté de Médecine de Reims le 14 Mai 1777 par* Jean-Claude Navier *sur l'usage de vin Champagne mousseux*... Paris & Reims. 1878

21. 1801 CHAPTAL *Traité théorique sur la culture de la vigne, avec l'art de faire le vin* Vol. I pp.134/7

22. 1808 PARMENTIER *Instructions sur les moyens de suppléer le sucre dans les principaux usages qu'on en fait pour la médecine et l'économie domestique*

23. 1810 PARMENTIER *Traité sur l'art de fabriquer les sirops et les conserves de raisins destinés à suppléer le sucre des colonies dans les principaux usages de l'économie domestique*

24. 1812 PARMENTIER *Aperçus des résultats obtenus de la fabrication des sirops et conserves de raisins dans le cours des années 1810 et 1811*

25. 1813 PARMENTIER *Nouvel aperçu des résultats obtenus de la fabrication des sirops et conserves de raisins dans le cours de l'année 1812*

26. 1813 A. JULLIEN *Manuel du Sommelier* p.94

27. 1815 LE GRAND D'AUSSY *Histoire de la vie privée des Français*

28. 1816 A. JULLIEN *Topographie de tous les vignobles connus*

29. 1822 A. JULLIEN *Topographie de tous les vignobles connus* 2e. ed

30. 1824 A. JULLIEN *Topography of all known vineyards* London Whittaker

31. 1825 COMTE LOUIS DE CHEVIGNÉ *La Champagne vengée, ou la louange du vin de Champagne* Paris Firmin Didot

32. 1827 CAVOLEAU *L'Œnologie française*

33. ABBÉ MANCEAU *Histoire de l'Abbaye d'Hautvillers* t.II p.47

34. LOUIS PARIS *Histoire de l'Abbaye d'Avenay*

35. 1841 *Physiologie du Vin de Champagne par deux buveurs d'eau* (Luzine et Bouviez) pp.24/25

36. 1845 MAX SUTAINE *Essai sur l'histoire du vin de Champagne*

37. CYRUS REDDING *A History and Description of Modern Wines*

38. 1852 THOMAS WALKER *The Art of Dining, or Gastronomy and Gastronomers* London Murray

39. 1858 VOLTAIRE *Siècle de Louis XIV* Paris ch. xxx, p.423

40. 1863 THOS.GEO.SHAW *Wine, the Vine and the Cellar* London

41. 1865 PERRIER *Mémoire sur le vin de Champagne* Paris Société des Bibliophiles, p.4

42. TOMES *The Champagne Country* London

43. 1870 CHARLES TOVEY *Champagne, its history, manufacture, properties, etc.* London

44. 1879 HENRY VIZETELLY *Facts about Champagne* London

45. 1882 HENRY VIZETELLY *A History of Champagne* London

46. 1883 BARON DE FOELCKERSAHMB-KROPPEN *Les archives de la gastronomie française* "La Champagne" Paris

47. 1884 *Œuvres du concours poétique sur le vin de Champagne* Epernay
48. 1897 ALBERT HARTSHORNE *Old English Glasses* London
49. A. BOURGEOIS *Le vin de Champagne sous Louis XIV et sous Louis XV* Paris
50. 1898 WEIMANN *Mannuel guide à l'usage des vignerons champenois* Epernay
51. 1905 ANDRÉ L. SIMON *History of the Champagne Trade in England* London
52. n.d PIERRE HAMP *La Peine des hommes II Le Vin de Champagne* Paris
53. 1908 ROCHE *Le Commerce des vins de Champagne sous l'ancien régime* Châlons-sur-Marne
54. 1922 DR CARLOS D'ESCHEVANNES *Contribution à l'histoire du Champagne* Reims Matot-Braine pp.66/7
55. 1925 MOREAU-BÉRILLON *Au pays du Champagne: Le vignoble, le vin* Reims
56. 1926 GRANT R. FRANCIS *Old English Glasses* London
57. 1930 MATHIEU *Le Champagne et la délimitation* Reims
58. 1932 GEORGE SAINTSBURY *Notes on a Cellar Book* London Macmillan
59. 1934 ANDRÉ L. SIMON *Champagne* Constable's Wine Library Series
60. 1937 LEJARD *Etiquettes de vin de Champagne* In *Revues des arts et métiers graphiques*, Paris
61. 1946 *Visages de la Champagne*, par MAURICE CATEL, GERMAINE MAILLET MAURICE HOLLANDE, RENÉ DRUART et JEAN-PAUL VAILLANT Paris
62. 1949 ANDRÉ L. SIMON *Champagne*, in the *Wines of the World Pocket Library* London Wine and Food Society
63. c. 1952 GEORGES CHAPPAZ *Le Vignoble et le vin de Champagne* Paris Larmat
64. 1952 MAURICE HOLLANDE *Connaissance du vin de Champagne* Paris
65. 1955 ALEXI: LICHINE *Wines of France* London Cassell pp.215/6
66. 1957 ANDRÉ L. SIMON *The Noble Grapes and Great Wines of France* London & New York McGraw-Hill
67. 1958 YVES GANDON *Champagne* Neuchâtel
68. 1959 MAURICE HOLLANDE *Sur les routes de la Champagne* Reims Michaud
69. 1960 LOUIS JACQUELIN et RENÉ POULAIN *Vignes et vins de France* Paris Flammarion
70. *Le Vigneron champenois* Vol. 77 pp.379, 390
71. *Stocks in merchants' Cellars on April 1st*
72. *Quantity of wine made from Marne vineyards*
73. *Sales of Champagne in France*

Index

A

Aisne (*département*) 16, 17, 99, 102, 105
Aisne (river) 40
Aix-la-Chapelle, Peace of 62
Ambonnay 19, 21, 22, 35, 117
America, United States of 131
Ardennes (*département*) 16
Argenteuil 41
Argentine 131
As You Like It 46
Aube (*département*) 16, 17, 102, 105, 109
Aubigny, Lord d' 48
Australia 131
Auteuil 40
Auxerre 16
Avenay 19, 22, 40, 48, 58, 117
Avesnes 43
Avize 19, 21, 22, 31, 63, 64
Ay-Champagne 19, 21, 22, 31, 39, 41, 42, 48, 55, 57, 82, 94, 107, 109, 114

B

Bagneux 40
Bagnolet 40
Bar-le-Duc 16
Bath 73
Baslieux 22
Baye 22
Beaumont-sur-Vesle 19, 21, 22
Beaunay 22
Beaune, Hospices de 54
Bedford, Earl of 49
Belgium 45, 132
Belval-sous-Châtillon 22
Bergères-les-Vertus 22
Béziers 105
Binson-Orquigny 22

Blanc de blancs 36
Bligny 22
Bodega 98
Boileau 55
Bollinger, Mme 74
Bonnivet 39
Bordeaux 99, 140
Bordeaux (wine) *see* Claret
Bottles 144–51
Bouilly 22
Boulogne-sur-Seine 40
Bourg-la-Reine 40
Boursault 23
Bouzy 19, 21, 23, 35, 40, 114
Branscourt 23
Brooks's 71–2
Brossette 55
Brouillet 23
Brugny-Vandancourt 23
Buckingham, Duke of 48, 157–8
Buenos Aires 102
Bulstrode, Sir Richard 59
Burgundy (province) 15, 42; (wine) 20, 40, 42, 42–3, 68, 69, 71, 101, 138
Butler, Samuel 50

C

Caen 59
Caesar, Julius 16
Café Royal 101
Cambrai 43
Cauroy 23
Cavoleau 17
Cavour restaurant 103
Châlons-sur-Marne 15, 16, 17, 18, 39, 64, 84, 109
Chambrecy 23
Champagne (province) 15–26, 38, 45; (région délimítée) 16–7, 28, 114–6
Champillon 19, 22, 23, 31, 114

Champlat-Boujacourt 23
Champvoisy 23
Chaptal, Jean-Antoine 17, 58, 65, 80–81, 82, 83
Charles II of England 48, 58, 66, 129, 157
Charles V, Emperor 39
Charonne 40
Chassins 23
Chastenay 40
Chesterfield, Earl of 62–63
Charlotte Elizabeth of Bavaria, Princess 55
Château-Thierry 16, 19
Châtillon-sur-Marne 23
Châtillon-sur-Seine 40
Chaumont 16
Chaumuzy 23
Chavot-Courcourt 23
Chenay 23
Chigny-les-Roses 18, 22, 23, 31, 39
Childers, Erskine 169
Chile 131
Chouilly 19, 22, 23, 31
Clamart 40
Claret 20, 40, 47, 71, 101, 138
Clichy-la-Garenne 40
Clicquot-Ponsardin, *Veuve* 43, 73–4
Clignancourt 40
Cognac 15
Coizard-Joches 23
Colbert 40, 41
Coligny 23
Comblizy 23
Comité Interprofessionel du Vin de Champagne (C.I.V.C.) 110, 134–5, 158–9, 161, 167
Compiègne 40
Congy 23
Corks 152–4
Cormicy 23

189

Maps

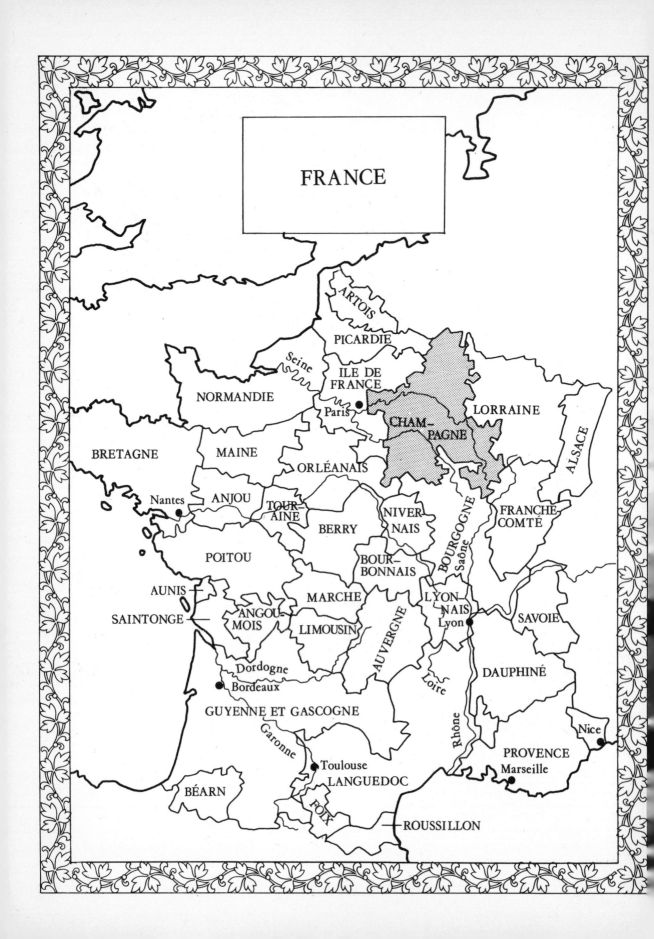

FRANCE

ARTOIS

PICARDIE

Seine

ILE DE
FRANCE

NORMANDIE

Paris

LORRAINE

CHAM-
PAGNE

ALSACE

BRETAGNE

MAINE

ORLÉANAIS

ANJOU

NIVER-
NAIS

FRANCHE-
COMTÉ

Nantes

TOUR-
AINE

BERRY

BOURGOGNE

Saône

POITOU

BOUR-
BONNAIS

AUNIS

MARCHE

LYON-
NAIS

SAINTONGE

ANGOU-
MOIS

LIMOUSIN

Lyon

SAVOIE

AUVERGNE

Dordogne

Loire

DAUPHINÉ

Bordeaux

GUYENNE ET GASCOGNE

Garonne

Rhône

Nice

PROVENCE

Toulouse

Marseille

BÉARN

LANGUEDOC

FOIX

ROUSSILLON

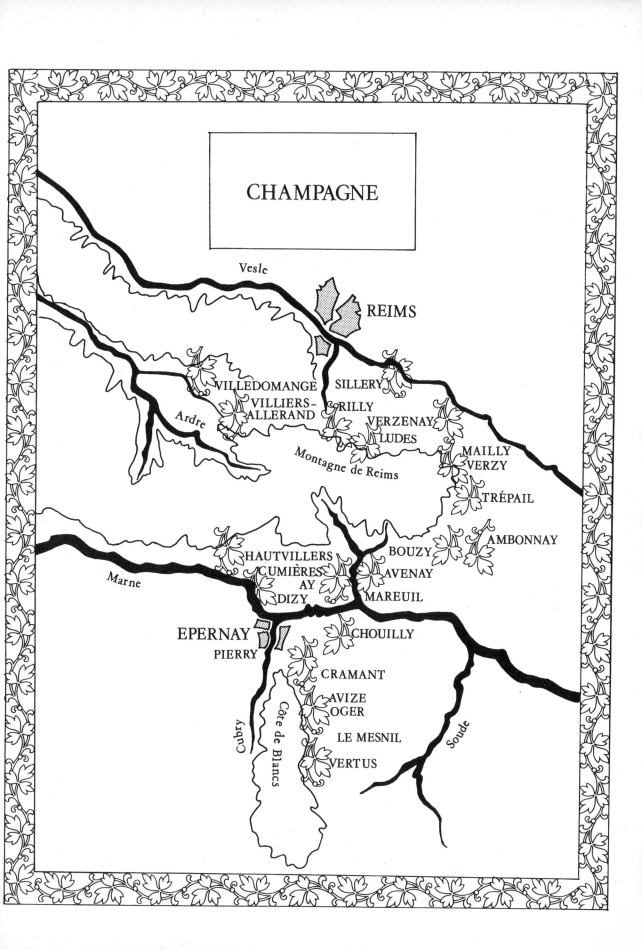